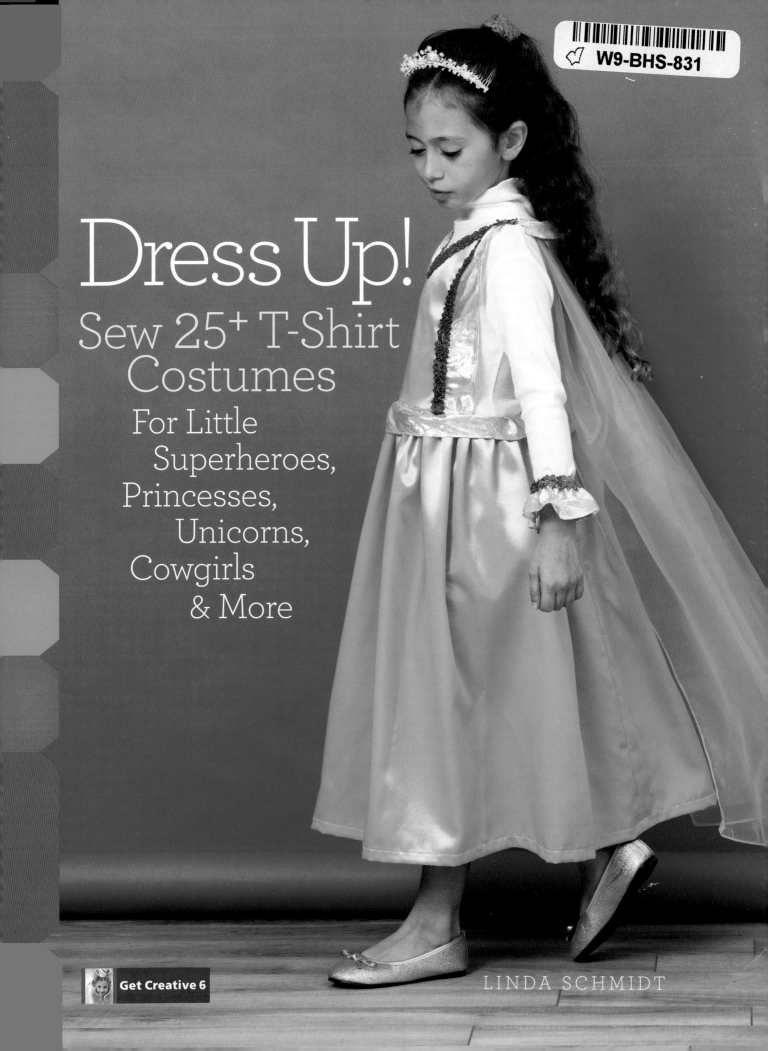

Dress Up!

Sew 25+ T-Shirt Costumes

For Little Superheroes, Princesses, Unicorns, Cowgirls & More

Get Creative 6

LINDA SCHMIDT

To my daughter, Monica Kay.
May you experience the multitude of love that returns
    when you share your talents with others.

Get Creative 6
An imprint of Mixed Media Resources
104 West 27th Street
New York, NY 10001

Connect with us on Facebook at **facebook.com/getcreative6**

SENIOR EDITOR
MICHELLE BREDESON

VICE PRESIDENT
TRISHA MALCOLM

CREATIVE DIRECTOR
DIANE LAMPHRON

CHIEF EXECUTIVE OFFICER
CAROLINE KILMER

PAGE LAYOUT
ARETA BUK

PRESIDENT
ART JOINNIDES

ASSOCIATE EDITOR
JACOB SEIFERT

CHAIRMAN
JAY STEIN

PROJECT COORDINATOR
ANAIS VILLA

PHOTOGRAPHER
JACK DEUTSCH

ILLUSTRATIONS
LINDA SCHMIDT

PRODUCTION
J. ARTHUR MEDIA

Library of Congress Cataloging-in-Publication Data
Names: Schmidt, Linda, author.
Title: Dress up! : sew 25+ T-shirt costumes for little superheroes,
    princesses, unicorns, cowgirls, and more / by Linda Schmidt.
Description: First edition. | New York : Get Creative 6, 2019. | Includes
    index.

Identifiers: LCCN 2019002428 | ISBN 9781640210479 (pbk.)
Subjects: LCSH: Children's costumes. | Sewing.
Classification: LCC TT633 .S3154 2019 | DDC 646.4/06--dc23
LC record available at https://lccn.loc.gov/2019002428

Manufactured in China

1 3 5 7 9 10 8 6 4 2

First Edition

CAT'S MEOW
(PAGE 70)

ABOUT THE AUTHOR

Growing up in Michigan, Linda Schmidt learned to sew, knit, and craft from her mother and grandmother. While working by day as a graphic designer and illustrator, she spent her spare time sewing clothes for herself, projects for the home, and endless costumes for her daughter (now a fashion designer for Ralph Lauren Polo). She now creates technical illustrations for knitting, sewing, and quilting books; teaches; and sells her own patterns on Ravelry (LOLfibernut) and Etsy (etsy.com/shop/ROFLhatfactory). She and her husband live in North Carolina.

ACKNOWLEDGMENTS

I praise God for the many miracles and people he has placed along my path. Thank you, Lord, for giving me parents and grandparents who saw their creative abilities as just a way of life. Through them, you inspired and instilled this creative passion that will be passed on and shared for your glory.

Thank you to my husband for his constant encouragement and indifference to multiple trips to the fabric store.

I'd like to thank Trisha Malcolm for trusting my talents to her idea and giving me this opportunity to fulfill a lifelong dream. I am very thankful to my editor, Michelle Bredeson, for guiding me on this journey. Amidst the fabric calamities, your calm professionalism kept my sanity and humor in intact. Being in the graphics field, I know exactly what goes into the production of a book. I most emphatically say thank you to Diane Lamphron, Jack Deutsch, Areta Buk, Anais Villa, everyone on the team for doing the hardest parts of all. I sincerely appreciate all the work you have done to produce something lasting and beautiful.

And to the little girls who modeled the costumes, you brought the true beauty to these dresses. Thank you for bringing back my treasured memories of spending time creating with my daughter.

THAT '70S GIRL
(PAGE 56)

Contents

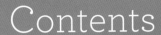

COLOR ME CUTE!
(PAGE 24)

Introduction

My parents and grandparents were fearless and perpetual makers of everything. In my youth, I grumbled when every fashion trend I begged for was met with, "We can't afford it, but we can make it." Their creative abilities taught me problem solving, perseverance, craftsmanship, and an appreciation for the talents we are all blessed to bless others with.

As a working mom, I didn't have time to make all the latest fashion trends for my daughter. But there were many special occasions, theatrical performances, and, of course, Halloween parties that required sewing something fabulous. Being the product of two artistic parents, my daughter's design requests were packed with imagination and detail. Much of her inspiration is reflected in this book.

When sewing for children, time, not imagination, seems to always be the concern. Starting with a T-shirt foundation is a major time-saver. The costumes in this book can be completed in a varied amount of time. Once you've gathered the materials, some can be easily created in a few hours and others a couple of days.

The T-shirt dress is the perfect approach for achieving the hardest issue of fit. There will be no wiggles or whines because her ball gown can actually fit as comfortably as her favorite T-shirt. Sewing buttonholes, zippers, or set-in sleeves can seem scary to some. But, fear not, none of these skills are needed. Just slip on the dress and dance.

I hope you and your little girl share the joy of choosing the materials and accessories. Then watch her eyes sparkle in excitement as you make her dress-up dreams come true.

SWEET ANGELICA
(PAGE 91)

T-Shirt Costumes 101

CHOOSING THE T-SHIRT AND FABRIC

The instructions in this book include detailed descriptions of the T-shirts, fabric, and other materials used to create the costumes. If you want to re-create the costumes shown in the photos, it is best to use the same materials.

SELECTING A T-SHIRT

A well-made cotton or cotton/polyester blend T-shirt that maintains its shape is the best choice. If the shirt has stretched or shrunk, it's not going to look any better as a dress than it did as a T-shirt. All except very lightweight T-shirts (which won't support the weight of the skirt) will work for these projects.

THINKING ABOUT SIZE

FOR THE SHIRT: Try the T-shirt on the child. If desired, choose a slightly larger shirt than usual to make the costume extra-comfortable. T-shirt sizes can vary; be sure to choose your project size based on your child's body measurements.

FOR THE SKIRT: The following chart provides standard body measurements for different sizes. Adjust the cutting length of the skirt for your child by measuring the length of a favorite skirt and using that measurement to cut the skirt fabric (remember to add 1" to 2" for seam and hem allowances). Each project indicates cutting lengths for the T-shirt and the skirt fabric.

MEASUREMENT CHART

SIZE	S (2/3)	M (4/5)	L (6/6X)	XL (7/8)
CHEST	22"	23"	25"	27"
ARMPIT TO WAIST	4"	4½"	5"	5½"
BACK WAIST LENGTH	8½"	9½"	10½"	12½"
WAIST TO KNEE	12"	13"	14"	16"

CHOOSING THE FABRIC

Most of the skirts in this book are made with woven fabrics, but knit fabrics can also be used (see page 9). Woven fabrics don't stretch and are generally very easy to work with, especially quilting cottons, which can be found in a variety of fabulous prints. Woven fabrics come in different weights, so select a light- to medium-weight cotton or silk, or a lightweight linen. If you add an overskirt, be sure to keep the underskirt fabric lighter weight than the overskirt. Bring the T-shirt with you when you shop for skirt fabric to match colors and test the skirt fabric weight against it.

CUTTING THE T-SHIRT AND FABRIC

Before cutting, wash, dry, and press the shirt and fabric.

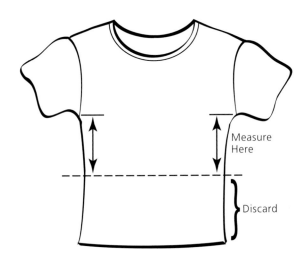

Measure Here

Discard

CUTTING THE T-SHIRT

Each project tells you where to cut the T-shirt to duplicate the look that is shown; adjust these measurements for the actual height of the child.

1. Lightly press the T-shirt.

2. Starting at the underarm seam on each side of the shirt, measure down the indicated cutting length and mark at the side seams with a fabric marker or chalk.

3. Use a ruler to draw a cutting line across the T-shirt connecting the two markings.

4. Cut along the marked line through both layers.

CUTTING THE SKIRT FABRIC

To duplicate the look of the dress as shown, follow the project cutting instructions.

• The length will be indicated; adjust this measurement to fit a shorter or taller child.

• To determine the cutting width, measure the circumference at the bottom edge of the cut T-shirt and multiply that measurement by 2, 2½, or 3 (2 for a moderately full skirt/ruffle and 3 for a very full skirt). In many cases, the result will be about 45", which is the width of many fabrics. If the result is greater than 45", you'll need to divide the cutting width in half, cut two fabric pieces, and seam them, right sides together, using a ½" seam allowance.

For example:
If the bottom circumference of the cut-off T-shirt is 20", and the instructions ask you to multiply it by 3 for a very full

skirt, the total width would be 60". That is wider than the usual 45" fabric width. In that case, divide the total width measurement in half and cut two fabric pieces 30" wide. Sew the edges together with a ½" seam. The total width measurement will actually be 59", but that will not make a noticeable difference in fullness. By dividing the width measurement in half, the dress seams will be placed evenly at the sides.

1. Press the fabric.

2. Trim the top edge as straight as possible. Cut the fabric so the length of the skirt is along the straight grain (parallel to the finished selvage edges) to ensure that the skirt hangs straight.

3. Measure and mark the desired length from the top edge at several intervals across the fabric width using fabric chalk, a fabric-marking pen, or straight pins. Use a long ruler to connect the markings.

4. Cut along the marked line.

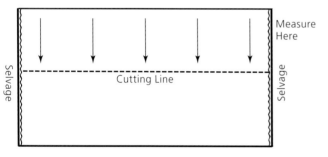

5. Repeat if you need a second width of fabric to obtain the desired skirt/ruffle fullness. Seam the two widths together along the straight grain.

TOOLS AND SUPPLIES

You won't need a lot of specialized tools to make these dresses, but the right ones will make sewing much easier and give you professional-looking results.

> **BASIC TOOL KIT**
> See project instructions for additonal tools.
>
> • matching thread
>
> • dressmaker's chalk or fabric-marking pen
>
> • fabric scissors
>
> • seam ripper
>
> • ruler and measuring tape
>
> • sewing machine, bobbins, and extra needles
>
> • straight pins
>
> • hand-sewing needles
>
> • iron and ironing board

SEWING MACHINE

As long as your sewing machine sews straight and zigzag stitches, you can make any dress in this book. Seams that need to stretch will benefit from a stretch stitch (or small zigzag), but for the most part a basic straight stitch is all you need.

NEEDLES
Start each project with a new needle. Keep a selection of sizes on hand for different weights and types of fabric (fine needles for lightweight fabrics like chiffon and tulle, thicker needles for heavyweight fabrics); the smaller the number size, the finer the needle. Many of the projects feature quilting cottons, and needle sizes 11/70 and 12/80 are suitable. A universal or sharp-point needle is suitable for most fabrics, especially wovens. If you're adding a knit fabric bottom to the T-shirt, use a ballpoint needle so the rounded tip will slip more easily through it.

If at any time your stitch appears irregular, change the needle and rethread the machine. It's surprising how these simple steps fix many stitch problems.

PRESSER FEET AND ATTACHMENTS
Almost every machine comes with an assortment of presser feet and you can usually purchase additional specialty feet. The **general-purpose foot** is ideal for most sewing, but there are a few feet that are very helpful for specific tasks.

The **narrow-rolled hem foot** allows the edge of the fabric to feed into the protruding spiral shapes that roll the edge over tightly before traveling under the straight stitches of the needle. This works best with lightweight or sheer fabrics.

Use a **zipper foot** to sew the bias tape close to edge of of the Busy Bee (see page 96) costume wings.

The shape of the **embroidery foot** allows it to move over satin stitches on appliqués or over fancy trims and ribbons.

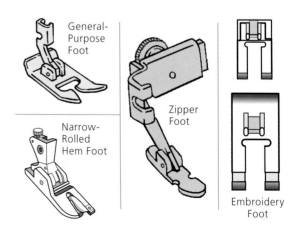

OTHER SEWING TOOLS

Insert **straight pins** every few inches, or even closer; the more you use, the less the fabrics will shift as you sew. Insert your pins perpendicular to the edge of the fabric so they're easy to remove as you sew.

Keep several **hand-sewing needles** on hand for tacking on trim and finishing work.

You'll need 7" or 8" **dressmaker's shears** for cutting T-shirts and fabric. **Smaller embroidery scissors** or thread snips are helpful for trimming seams and clipping threads. **Pinking shears** are a great way to trim and edge-finish seams that might otherwise ravel.

Accurate measuring is important. A 2" or 3" wide **transparent ruler** is ideal for measuring and marking straight cutting lines, while a **tape measure** can measure around curves.

You can mark cutting lines and length and width measurements directly on most fabrics with **dressmaker's chalk** or **fabric markers**, although you should test first on a scrap or corner. Chalk lines can be brushed off and lines made with water-soluble markers will disappear when water is applied.

Have a **seam ripper** on hand—just in case!

NOTIONS

It's fun to have an assortment of trims and novelties. Each project specifies the notions needed to make the garment, but when you're out and about and spot great trims, pick them up. You'll use them eventually, and you never know what might make the perfect finishing touch.

THREAD

Cotton/polyester blend thread is suitable for most sewing; 100% polyester also works because it stretches. Avoid 100% cotton for knit fabrics because it doesn't stretch. Always keep white and black thread on hand.

BASIC SEWING STITCHES

The following machine stitches are all you need to make the dresses in this book.

Backstitch for about 1" at the beginning and end of each seam to keep the thread ends from unraveling.

Basting, the longest machine stitch, has two purposes: it holds layers together temporarily and it gathers a length of fabric.

An **edgestitch** is a permanent stitch, visible on the right side, stitched as close as possible to a folded edge.

Staystitching is a row of straight stitches through a single layer of fabric, usually done along a curved edge (or along the straight edge of a knit fabric) within the seam allowance to prevent stretching. If the T-shirt you are working with tends to stretch a lot, staystitch the bottom edge after you cut it.

A **topstitch** is a decorative stitch that is meant to be seen; embroidery or contrast-color threads make it even more visible.

The **zigzag stitch** is particularly important when working with knitted fabrics because it stretches. Use a narrow

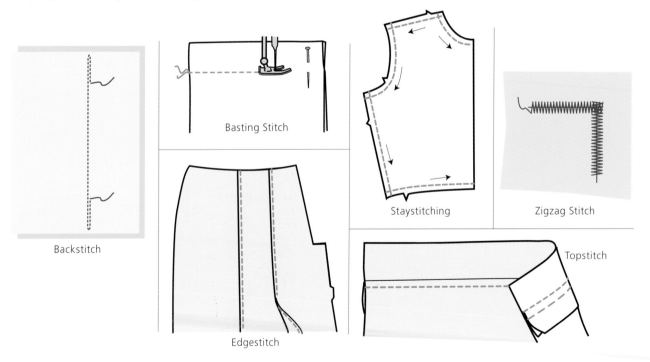

Backstitch

Basting Stitch

Staystitching

Zigzag Stitch

Edgestitch

Topstitch

zigzag when sewing the skirt to the bottom of the T-shirt. It is also used as an edge finish to prevent raveling, and to secure appliqués. Vary the length and width for different results; a shorter zigzag looks like a satin stitch and is perfect for stitching appliqués, while a wider stitch is better for decorative stitching.

BASIC SEWING TECHNIQUES

There are certain basic sewing techniques that you will use over and over again as you sew the projects in this book. Unless otherwise indicated, all seams in this book are sewn with straight stitches set at 8 to 12 stitches per 1", and ½" seam allowances.

PRESSING

Pressing is the key to successful sewing. Press every seam you sew to ensure flat, smooth seams.

To press, smooth the seam with your hands, press the iron onto the seam, and then lift the iron, move it to a new section, and repeat. Press every seam flat right after you sew it. Unless otherwise specified, press both seam allowances to one side and generally to the back of the garment. Pressing is particularly important when sewing the skirt bottoms to the knit shirts. Don't move the iron back and forth (that's ironing, and should only be done on flat fabric and finished garments).

WORKING WITH KNIT FABRICS

The great thing about knit fabrics is that they don't have to fit perfectly because they stretch. Because these T-shirt dresses all have knit tops, you don't have to worry about zippers or buttonholes.

Here are some tips for sewing knits. It's best to use a stretch stitch. If your machine doesn't have a stretch stitch, don't worry; use a narrow zigzag stitch instead, and follow these tips:

• Knit fabric stretches, and so should the stitching.

• If the cut edge of the T-shirt rolls, spray it with starch and press it gently.

• Install a new, ballpoint needle in your machine before beginning work.

• Stitch with a longer stitch length (9 per 1").

• Gently stretch the seam as you stitch.

• If you have a serger, use it to stitch and edge-finish knit fabrics at the same time.

STITCHING WOVEN SKIRTS TO KNIT TOPS

In most instances, you'll be stitching a woven bottom to a knit top, using either a stretch or a zigzag stitch.

1. Staystitch (see page 8) the bottom edge of the T-shirt within the seam allowance. Take care to avoid stretching the fabric.

2. Use many pins to hold the layers together and ensure that the knit layer doesn't distort during stitching.

3. Every few inches, stop and lift the presser foot as you stitch to avoid distortion and fabric creeping.

WORKING WITH SHEER FABRICS

Several dresses are made with sheer fabrics like chiffon, organza, and tulle. Here are a few tips that will make cutting and sewing these special fabrics easier.

• Pin or tape sheer fabrics to a cutting mat or a piece of foamcore to minimize slippage while cutting. Because the fabric will be gathered, small imperfections in cutting will be hidden in the layers.

• Start with a new, finer needle (try size 9/60 or 10/70) and set your machine for a short stitch length.

• Hold the thread ends as you begin sewing.

• Stop sewing every 6" and leave the needle down; lift the presser foot to release any tension in the fabric. Continue sewing, taking care not to push or pull the fabric.

A **French seam** is a seam and seam finish all in one and it's ideal for sheer fabrics. Allow a ⅝" seam allowance.

1. Sew a ⅜" seam with the wrong sides together. Trim the seam allowance to ⅛".

2. Turn the seam inside out so the right sides are together and the narrow seam allowance is sandwiched between the fabric layers; press.

3. Sew the seam again using a ¼" seam allowance to encase the raw edges. Turn the garment right side out and press.

Refer to the narrow hem (see page 10) for the best way to hem chiffon and organza, which can shift as you sew. Tulle should be left unhemmed.

TURNING CORNERS

Slow down as you approach a corner. Stop with the needle down when you are ½" from the edge of the fabric. Lift the presser foot and pivot the fabric. Lower the presser foot and continue stitching.

For heavier weight fabric, round the corner by taking two diagonal stitches.

TRIMMING, CLIPPING, AND NOTCHING SEAM ALLOWANCES

Before seam finishing, trim, clip, and notch as needed to reduce bulk and ease the seam allowance so it lies flat. Take special care not to cut through the stitching when clipping or notching. On tight curves, clip or notch about every ½"; on gentler curves every 1".

Trim the seam allowances to about ¼" to reduce bulk.

Clip small snips into the seam allowances of inwardly curved seams and cut out small notches of outwardly curves seams.

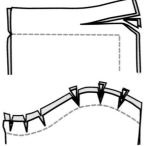

CLEAN-FINISHING SEAM ALLOWANCES

It's a good idea to clean-finish the seam allowances so they don't ravel and create a rat's nest of threads on the inside when laundered.

Pinked Seam Finish: Trim away the excess seam allowance with pinking shears. The zigzag-cut edge won't ravel and makes a soft, comfortable edge after washing. If the fabric ravels a lot, stitch ¼" from each raw edge before you pink the edges.

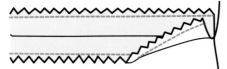

Zigzag Seam Finish: Press the seam open and stitch a narrow zigzag along the cut edge of each seam allowance. On lightweight fabrics, you can zigzag the seam allowances together.

Overlock Finish: If you have a serger, you already know it's the quickest and easiest way to finish seam allowances. And it trims the seam allowance as it overlocks the cut edge.

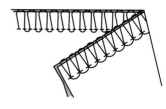

NARROW-HEMMING

Because most of these projects are casual dresses, machine hemming is the way to go. And in most instances, unless otherwise indicated, a narrow hem is the easiest and most suitable. Here are three ways to do it; Method 3 is particularly suited to sheers.

Method 1: Trim the hem allowance to ½" and zigzag or overlock the cut edge. Press the hem allowance to the wrong side and machine edgestitch it in place.

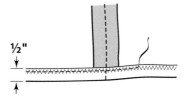

Method 2: Trim the hem allowance to ½". Press ¼" to the wrong side and then ¼" again. Machine edgestitch close to the inner fold.

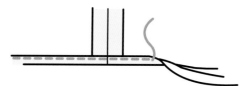

Method 3: Mark the hemline and trim the hem allowance to ½". Press the hem allowance to the wrong side on the marked hemline. With the right side up, narrow zigzag along the fabric fold. Carefully trim away the excess hem allowance.

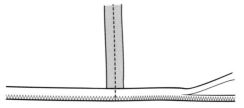

GATHERING

Gathering is a way of sewing a larger width of fabric to a smaller width with a series of soft folds. It's also used to make ruffles.

When joining two or more strips together to obtain the desired width (see page 6), mark both sections to ensure evenly distributed gathers.

Many projects require gathering, and gathering uses a lot of thread, so make extra bobbins with white thread. You don't want to have to stop mid-project to wind a new bobbin.

MARKING FOR GATHERING
For most of the projects in this book, you will be gathering the top edge of the skirts to the bottom edges of the T-shirts. The key to even gathering is careful marking.

1. Fold the T-shirt in half lengthwise to find the center front and center back.

2. If the skirt has one seam, make it the center back; if there are two seams, make them the side seams. Fold the skirt in half and in half again, positioning the seams as desired.

3. Make a chalk mark or insert a straight pin at all the folds on the T-shirt and on the skirt to mark the center front, center back, and sides (or halfway between the centers).

MAKING RUFFLES
Straight ruffles are softly gathered rectangular strips of fabric. Variety is created in the way they are attached to the garment.

BASIC STRAIGHT RUFFLE
This can be a single layer that's narrow-hemmed on the lower edge (see below left) or a double layer ruffle (see below right). The upper edge of both a single- and a double-layer ruffle is gathered as described above and stitched to the garment.

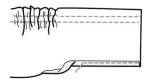 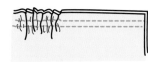

APPLYING FLAT TRIM
You can always handstitch trim in place, but it's so quick and easy to stitch it by machine.

1. Secure the trim in the desired location with lots of pins, basting tape, or even fabric adhesive.

2. If the trim is narrow, simply run one row of straight machine stitches down the center. This typically works with rickrack, soutache, and narrow ribbon.

3. If the trim is wider than ¼", machine stitch both long edges. To avoid puckers, stitch both edges in the same direction.

4. To apply flat trim or edging to the hem of a garment, position the wrong side of the garment over the edge of the trim and edgestitch close to the fold.

MAKING FABRIC SASH BELTS OR HAIR TIES
Depending on the weight of the fabric, you can make a single-layer or a double-layer sash or hair tie. Both are suitable for a little girl's dress. To determine the best length, tie a tape measure or fabric scrap around the child's waist (or around her hairline) and use that as a guide. The width will vary depending on the style of the dress, but most fabric sashes are between 1½" and 4" wide.

MAKING A DOUBLE FABRIC SASH BELT
Length: desired length + 1"
Width: double the desired width + 1"

1. Fold the fabric with the right sides together. Stitch the short edges and long edge, leaving a 3" opening for turning on the long edge.

2. Trim the seam allowances and turn the sash right side out. Press the seam allowances at the opening to the wrong side.

3. Edgestitch all around the sash, closing the opening in the stitching. If desired, stitch the narrow ends at an angle. Trim the ends.

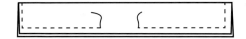

WORKING WITH THE TEMPLATES
While none of the costume designs requires a pattern, a few feature elements that require templates, which are found on page 128. Some designs use a template for an appliqué cutout. Other designs require you to make a paper cutout template to use as a tool to mark a scalloped or pointed edge. A stiffer cardstock might be helpful for those cases that require multiple tracings. Some templates you create by placing copy/printer paper on the T-shirt and tracing the armhole and neckline. Though the illustrations provided to make some templates may give the impression that precision is necessary, they are merely guides to follow. Once a shape is cut and the fabric sewn, imperfect circles and curved edges smooth out in appearance.

To use your template, start by photocopying the page on which it appears at the same size (100%). In most cases, you'll need to copy it once, but it may be used multiple times. Cut out the photocopied template and position it on your fabric or special material. Pin or tape it in place before cutting. With a more complicated template, such as the dragon (see page 134), do not cut the template out first. Position the photocopied image over the material and cut through both the paper and the material. Depending on the material, a sharp craft knife will work better than scissors. ■

Being a
PRINCESS—
or at least
looking the
part—is a
DREAM
come true.

Royal Treatment

Royal Treatment

This sumptuous gown oozes royal style with velvet, organza, tulle, and rhinestones. Your little princess will be thrilled to make her grand entrance wearing it.

Instructions are for sizes Small (Medium, Large, Extra-Large). Select the size to sew based on the closest matching chest measurement in the chart on page 6. All seam allowances are ½" unless otherwise noted.

WHAT YOU'LL NEED
• Basic tool kit (see page 7)

• Craft knife

• Narrow-rolled hem foot

• Hot-glue gun and glue sticks

• T-shirt: white, long sleeve

• White chiffon double-seam ruffled trim (see yardage chart at right)

• ¼ yard lightweight iron-on interfacing

• Multicolored round glue-on rhinestones

• Gem glue

For the skirt and front panel:
• Purple glitter velvet (see yardage chart at right)

For the train and hip bustles:
• Purple glitter organza (see yardage chart at right)

58"-wide fabric	S (2/3)	M (4/5)	L (6/6x)	XL (7/8)
Purple velvet	1½ yards	1½ yards	1¾ yards	1¾ yards
Purple organza	1¾ yards	1¾ yards	2 yards	2 yards

⅜"-wide trim	S (2/3)	M (4/5)	L (6/6x)	XL (7/8)
White chiffon ruffle	3¾ yards	4 yards	4½ yards	4¾ yards

PREPARING THE T-SHIRT
1. Lay the T-shirt out, mark 4 (4½, 5, 5½)" down from each underarm seam, and follow the cutting instructions on page 6. Mark at the center front and back.

SEWING THE BODICE
2. To create the center bodice panel, cut two pieces of the velvet fabric 4½" wide. To determine the cutting length, measure from the center front of the neckline to the waistline, then add 1". Cut the interfacing 3½" wide by the same fabric length less 1". On the wrong side of the velvet fabric, follow the pressing time instructions and iron on the interfacing. With the right sides of the two velvet pieces together, sew a ½" seam on two edges to create a long tube. Turn the panel right side out and press flat. Fold the fabric in ½" on one end of the tube and press flat. Topstitch the edge. Sew down the center of the double-seam chiffon trim to attach to each side of the panel. Fold the ruffle toward the outsides of the panel and topstitch the chiffon trim to the edges. Glue rhinestones down the center, but leave ½" at the bottom unembellished to sew on the skirt. Sew the top edge of the panel to the T-shirt, touching the neckline. Baste the bottom edge to the waistline.

3. Measure the circumference of the neckline and add 1" to determine the cutting length of the chiffon ruffle trim. Starting at the back, using a narrow zigzag stitch, sew the trim around the T-shirt neckline. Cover the top edge of the bodice panel stitches, overlap, and turn under the trim rough ends.

4. Create shoulder puffs to be sewn from the center front of the sleeve armhole to the center back of the sleeve armhole: Measure and cut two pieces of chiffon trim to that length. Cut two pieces of the organza 5" wide by twice the length of the trim. Fold the organza in half lengthwise and sew two rows of basting stitches for gathering; sew one row ¼" from the edge and the second row ¼" below that. Pull the threads and gather the organza to match the length of the trim. Sew the organza ruffle to the center of the chiffon trim. Fold the chiffon trim in half to sandwich the organza gathering seam inside. Topstitch along the trim edge. Handstitch the shoulder puffs to the seams around each sleeve armhole.

SEWING THE SKIRT
5. Measure the circumference of the T-shirt at the chest and multiply times 3 to determine the skirt velvet fabric cutting width. If the width measurement is wider than the fabric width, divide that number in half. Then cut two fabric pieces and sew them together. This creates two side seams and prevents an awkward seam placement. Use the chart on the next page to cut the skirt length.

	S (2/3)	M (4/5)	L (6/6x)	XL (7/8)
Skirt length	22"	24"	26"	30"

6. Finish-stitch along the top and bottom edges. On the waistline edge, sew two rows of basting stitches for gathering; sew one row ¼" from the edge and the second row ¼" below that. Create a narrow hem (see page 10) on the bottom edge. Measure 6" up from the hem and sew on the chiffon ruffle. With right sides together, sew and finish-stitch the side edges to create a back seam. Fold to divide the skirt into quarters and mark the sides, front, and back.

ATTACHING THE SKIRT TO THE T-SHIRT
7. Pull threads to gather the skirt waistline. With right sides together, using a narrow zigzag stitch, matching marks, sew the skirt to the T-shirt waistband. Remove all gathering stitches.

8. To create the hip bustles, measure from the edge of the bodice panel in front to a similar distance around the back of the T-shirt and cut two pieces of chiffon trim to that length. Cut two pieces of the organza 15" wide by twice the length of the trim. Fold the organza in half lengthwise. On the cut edges, sew two rows of basting stitches for gathering; sew one row ¼" from the edge and the second row ¼" below that. Pull the threads and gather the organza to match the length of the trim. Sew the organza ruffle to the center of the chiffon trim. Fold the trim in half to sandwich the organza seam inside. Topstitch along the trim edge. Handstitch the bustles around the waistline at the hip. Remove all gathering stitches.

SEWING THE CAPE
9. Keep the organza fabric at the 58" width. Determine the length by measuring from the collar to the floor, then add 8". Narrow-roll a hem on all four edges. Fold over and sew the top edge to create a 4" stand-up collar. Sew two rows of basting stitches for gathering; one row next to the collar fold seam and one ¼" below that. Under the chiffon ruffle, along the back shoulders and neck seam, gather and handstitch the cape to the T-shirt. Remove all gathering threads. ■

You won't mind having this cute CRITTER around the HOUSE.

Miss Mouse

Miss Mouse

A fabulously poufy skirt, bold buttons, and sweet eyelet trim add up to the perfect outfit for a cartoon diva. Red and white is a classic look, but feel free to use pink if your little mouse prefers it.

Instructions are for sizes Small (Medium, Large, Extra-Large). Select the size to sew based on the closest matching chest measurement in the chart on page 6. All seam allowances are ½" unless otherwise noted.

WHAT YOU'LL NEED

- Basic tool kit (see page 7)
- T-shirt: red, puffy short sleeve
- ¾ yard 2" white ruffled eyelet lace trim
- 2 large white buttons
- 1½ yards 1" white satin ribbon

For the skirt:
- Red polka-dot quilt cotton (see yardage chart at right)
- Black tulle (see yardage chart at right)

44"-wide fabric	S (2/3)	M (4/5)	L (6/6x)	XL (7/8)
Red polka-dot	1 yard	1 yard	1 yard	1¼ yards

54"-wide fabric	S (2/3)	M (4/5)	L (6/6x)	XL (7/8)
Black tulle	3¾ yards	4 yards	4¼ yards	4½ yards

PREPARING THE T-SHIRT

1. Lay the T-shirt out flat, measure and mark 3½ (4, 4½, 5)" down from each underarm seam, and follow the cutting instructions on page 6. Mark the center front and center back.

2. Measure the circumference of the neckline and add 1" to determine the length to cut the eyelet trim. Starting at the back of the neck, using a narrow zigzag stitch, sew the trim ¼" from the edge of the T-shirt neckline. Overlap and turn under the trim ends. Avoid stretching the neckline as you sew.

SEWING THE SKIRT

3. To determine the cutting width for the waistband, measure the circumference of the T-shirt at the chest and add 2". Cut the polka-dot fabric waistband length at 8". With right sides facing, sew the short edges together to create the center back seam. Fold in half lengthwise, with wrong sides together, and then baste and finish the edges. Fold the waistband to divide into quarters and mark the sides and front.

4. For the skirt, measure the circumference of the T-shirt at the chest and multiply by 3 to determine the polka-dot fabric cutting width. If the width measurement is wider than the fabric width, divide that number in half, then cut two fabric pieces and sew them together. This creates two side seams and prevents an awkward seam placement. Use the chart below to cut the skirt length.

	S (2/3)	M (4/5)	L (6/6x)	XL (7/8)
Skirt length	11"	12"	13"	15"

5. Finish-stitch along the top and bottom edges. With right sides facing, fold and sew the sides to create the back seam of the skirt. On the waistline edge, sew two rows of basting stitches for gathering; sew one row ¼" from the edge and the second row ¼" below that. Fold to divide the skirt into quarters and mark the sides and front. Narrow-hem (see page 10) the bottom edge of the skirt.

6. Pull the basting threads to gather the skirt waistline. With right sides together, sew the skirt 1" from the folded edge of the waistband. Remove all the gathering stitches.

7. To make two tulle pieces, measure the circumference of the T-shirt at the chest and multiply by 3 to determine the fabric cutting length. Fold one piece of tulle twice lengthwise to create four fabric layers. Sew two rows of basting stitches for gathering; sew one row ¼" from the edge and the second row ¼" below that.

TIP
To add more fluff to the tulle skirt layers, sew the layers upside down. This allows the tulle fabric to fold over the seam that it was sewn on with.

TIP
To keep the large buttons from drooping on the thin T-shirt, add small buttons behind them on the inside of the T-shirt and sew them together.

Cut the width in the chart below, measuring from the basting seam. Repeat for the second tulle piece. Fold to divide into quarters and mark the sides and front.

	S (2/3)	M (4/5)	L (6/6x)	XL (7/8)
Tulle width	10"	11"	12"	13"

8. Pull the basting threads to gather. Under the polka-dot fabric layer, pin and match the sides and center markings on the waistband. Starting at the back, sew one tulle piece flat to the waistband. To alternate the open short edges between the pieces, start at the side seam and sew the second piece of tulle beneath the first tulle piece. Fluff and separate the fabric layers for fullness.

ATTACHING THE SKIRT TO THE T-SHIRT
9. With right sides together and a ½" seam, sew the skirt waistband to the T-shirt. Use a narrow zigzag stitch and match the sides, front, and back marks.

ADDING THE FINISHING TOUCHES
10. Tie a white ribbon sash around the waist. Measure the ribbon to the desired length and cut at an angle to prevent the ends from fraying. Hand-tack it to the waistband at the side seams.

11. Sew the buttons onto the T-shirt front as shown in the photo. ■

19

This pretty
pink
TUTU is
"en POINTE"!
Tiny Dancer

Tiny Dancer

Many girls dream of twirling and leaping across the stage.
A little satin and tulle can make that wish come true.

Instructions are for sizes Small (Medium, Large, Extra-Large). Select the size to sew based on the closest matching chest measurement in the chart on page 6. All seam allowances are ½" unless otherwise noted.

WHAT YOU'LL NEED

• Basic tool kit (see page 7)

• T-shirt: white, sleeveless

• ½ yard 59"-wide fuchsia silky charmeuse

• White netting (see yardage chart at right)

• Pink tulle (see yardage chart at right)

• 2"-wide pink ruffled eyelet trim (see yardage chart at right)

• 3 (3, 4, 4) white shank buttons

54"-wide fabric	S (2/3)	M (4/5)	L (6/6x)	XL (7/8)
Pink tulle	3¾ yards	4 yards	4¼ yards	4½ yards
White nylon netting	2 yards	2 yards	2¼ yards	2¼ yards

2"-wide trim	S (2/3)	M (4/5)	L (6/6x)	XL (7/8)
Pink eyelet	1¼ yards	1¼ yards	1½ yards	1½ yards

PREPARING THE T-SHIRT

1. Press the T-shirt out flat, measure and mark 4 (4½, 5, 5½)" down from each underarm seam, and follow the cutting instructions on page 6. Mark at the center front and center back.

SEWING THE BODICE

2. To make the front panel, cut the fuchsia charmeuse fabric 4½" wide by the length measured from the front neckline to the waistline plus 1". Fold in half lengthwise, right sides together, and sew a ½" seam to create a long tube. Turn inside out and press flat. Fold the fabric in ½" on one end of the tube and press flat. Topstitch the panel end closed. Sew eyelet trim on each side. Pin the panel to the T-shirt at the center front and sew across the neckline and baste-stitch across the waistline edge. Through the T-shirt and panel layers, hand-sew on the buttons evenly spaced down the center.

3. Measure the neckline from the edges of the panel around the back of the neck. Cut eyelet trim to the neckline measurement and add 1". Cut two strips of netting 4" wide by 2 times the neckline measurement. Fold lengthwise and press. Sew two rows of basting stitches for gathering along that folded edge; sew one row ¼" from the edge and the second row ¼" below that. Pull the threads to gather and sew the netting to the wrong side of the eyelet lace trim edge. Using a narrow zigzag stitch, starting from one side of the panel, turn the raw ends under slightly and sew the trim to the T-shirt.

SEWING THE SKIRT

4. Measure the circumference of the T-shirt at the chest and multiply by 1½ to determine the charmeuse fabric cutting width. Use the chart below to cut the length for the underskirt.

	S (2/3)	M (4/5)	L (6/6x)	XL (7/8)
Underskirt length	8½"	9"	9½"	11"

5. Finish-stitch along the top and bottom edges. With right sides facing, fold and sew the sides to make the back seam of the underskirt. On the waistline edge, sew two rows of basting stitches for gathering; sew one row ¼" from the edge and the second row ¼" below that. Fold to divide the underskirt into quarters and mark the sides, front, and back. Create a narrow hem (see page 10) on the bottom edge.

6. To make two tulle pieces and one netting piece, measure the circumference of the T-shirt at the chest and multiply by 3 to determine the fabric cutting length. Fold one piece of tulle lengthwise twice to create four fabric layers. Sew two rows of basting stitches for gathering; sew one row ¼ " from the folded edge and the second row ¼ " below that. Cut the width in the chart below, measuring from the basting seam. Repeat for the second tulle piece and the netting piece. Fold each piece to divide into quarters and mark the center and side seams.

	S (2/3)	M (4/5)	L (6/6x)	XL (7/8)
Tulle and netting width	10"	11"	12"	13"

7. Pull the basting threads to gather. Pin and match the sides and center markings. Starting at the back, sew one tulle piece flat to the underskirt below the double-baste stitching on the underskirt edge. To alternate the open short edges between the pieces, start at the side seam and then sew the second piece of tulle beneath the first tulle piece. Start at the other side seam to sew the netting piece beneath both tulle pieces. Fluff and separate the fabric layers for fullness.

ATTACHING THE SKIRT TO THE T-SHIRT
8. Pull threads to gather the skirt waistline. With right sides together, sew the skirt to the T-shirt, making sure to catch the top layer of tulle within the seam. Use a narrow zigzag stitch, matching sides, front, and back marks. Remove all gathering stitches. ■

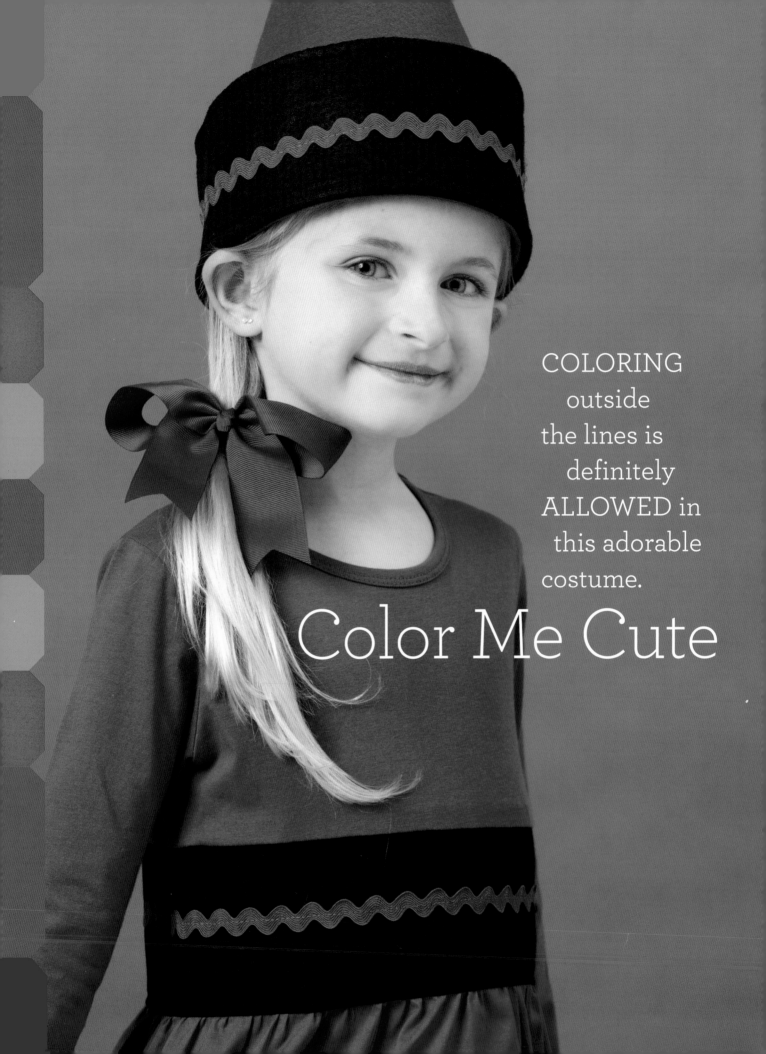

COLORING outside the lines is definitely ALLOWED in this adorable costume.

Color Me Cute

Color Me Cute

The only thing more fun than coloring is being a crayon!
Get together a group of little ones in all different colors for
a box full of fun. A felt hat tops off this creative look.

Instructions are for sizes Small (Medium, Large, Extra-Large). Select the size to sew based on the closest matching chest measurement in the chart on page 6. All seam allowances are ½" unless otherwise noted.

WHAT YOU'LL NEED
• Basic tool kit (see page 7)

• String and marking pen

• T-shirt: blue, long sleeve

For the skirt:
• Blue cotton fabric (see yardage chart at right)

• ¾ yard black cotton fabric

• ⅝" blue jumbo rickrack trim (see yardage chart at right)

• 6" x 12" double fusible web

• 2" white block-letter iron-on transfers

For the hat:
• 26" x 13" blue craft felt

• 25" x 9" black craft felt

44"-wide fabric	S (2/3)	M (4/5)	L (6/6x)	XL (7/8)
Blue cotton	½ yard	½ yard	¾ yard	¾ yard

⅝" trim	S (2/3)	M (4/5)	L (6/6x)	XL (7/8)
Bue jumbo rickrack	2¼ yards	2½ yards	2¾ yards	2¾ yards

PREPARING THE T-SHIRT
1. Lay the T-shirt out flat, measure and mark 1½ (2, 2½, 3)" down from each underarm seam, and follow the cutting instructions on page 6. Mark the center front and center back.

SEWING THE BODICE
2. To determine the fabric cutting width to make the waistband, measure the circumference of the T-shirt at the chest and add 2". Cut the black cotton fabric length at 5". Sew the rickrack trim to the horizontal center of the black fabric. With right sides together, sew the short edges together to create the center back seam.

3. Fold the waistband to divide it into quarters and mark the sides and front. With the right sides of the T-shirt and waistband together, sew a ½" seam, using a narrow zigzag stitch and matching the side, front, and back marks.

SEWING THE SKIRT
4. Measure the circumference of the T-shirt at the chest and multiply by 1½ to determine the desired cutting width of the blue cotton skirt. Refer to the chart below for the cutting length.

	S (2/3)	M (4/5)	L (6/6x)	XL (7/8)
Skirt length	14"	15"	17"	19"

5. To determine the fabric cutting width to make the hem band, match the skirt width and cut the black cotton fabric length at 9". Fold the band in half lengthwise and sew with wrong sides together to create a double-thick hem band. Sew the rickrack trim to the horizontal center of the band. With right sides together, sew the hem band to the bottom edge of the skirt. Fold the skirt in half to determine the skirt center front.

6. To create the crayon label appliqué, cut a piece of black cotton fabric 5" wide by the length of the skirt minus 4". On the wrong side of the fabric, follow the product instructions and iron on the double fusible web. Make a 5" circle paper template to mark and cut rounded ends to the black label shape. Center and space the block letters evenly on the right side of the black label shape. Double-check your spelling and follow the product instructions to iron the letters to the appliqué. Peel off the double fusible-web backing, center, and iron the appliqué to the centerline of the skirt.

7. With right sides facing, sew the short edges of the skirt together to create the back seam. On the waistline edge, sew two rows of basting stitches for gathering; sew one row ¼" from the edge and the second row ¼" below that. Fold to divide the skirt into quarters and mark the sides, front, and back.

Paper Template

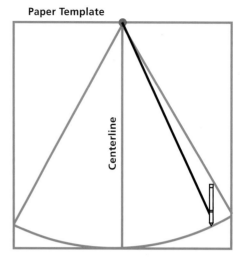

Centerline

Folded Fabric

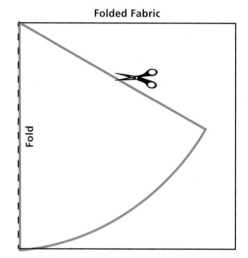

Fold

ATTACHING THE SKIRT TO THE T-SHIRT

8. Pull the basting threads to gather the skirt waistline. With right sides together, sew the T-shirt waistband and skirt together, matching the side, front, and back marks. Remove all the gathering stitches.

SEWING THE HAT

9. To create the crayon hat template, cut a paper 13" square. Referring to Figure A, mark the centerline. With a 13" string attached to a marking pen, draw a curve. Draw straight lines from the center point to where the paper edge meets the curve mark. Cut out the cone-shaped template. Fold the blue felt fabric in half to form a 13" square. Align the angled edge of the template along the folded fabric edge and cut out the cone shape. Sew the side edges together to form a point. Turn the cone right sides out, not completely turning the pointed end to create a blunt tip.

10. For the hat's brim, measure the child's head circumference, then add 3" to determine the cutting width of the black felt fabric. Cut the fabric length at 9". Sew the short edges together to create a circle. Fold the band in half and sew the edges together to create a double-thick brim. Sew the rickrack trim to the horizontal center of the brim. Place the brim inside the cone. Pin the edges together, right side of the brim facing the wrong side of the hat. Sew the brim to the bottom edge of the hat. Roll the brim up and right side out. ■

Figure A

It's a beautiful
tale of
SEQUINS
and sparkly
TULLE.

Under the Sea

Under the Sea

There's something fishy going on, but this project will go swimmingly with dotted metallic fabric taking the place of scales. A comfortable tail allows this cute mermaid to walk and skip.

Instructions are for sizes Small (Medium, Large, Extra-Large). Select the size to sew based on the closest matching chest measurement in the chart on page 6. All seam allowances are ½" unless otherwise noted.

WHAT YOU'LL NEED

• Basic tool kit (see page 7)

• T-shirt: purple, puffy short sleeve

For the bodice:

• ⅞" turquoise stretch sequin trim (see yardage chart at right)

• Iron-on seashell appliqué

For the skirt:

• Turquoise dotted metallic nylon stretch fabric (see yardage chart at right)

• 1¾ yards 58"-wide turquoise glitter tulle

43"-wide fabric	S (2/3)	M (4/5)	L (6/6x)	XL (7/8)
Metallic nylon stretch	¾ yard	1 yard	1 yard	1¼ yards
⅞"-wide trim	**S (2/3)**	**M (4/5)**	**L (6/6x)**	**XL (7/8)**
Sequin stretch	1¼ yards	1¼ yards	1½ yards	1½ yards

PREPARING THE T-SHIRT

1. Lay the T-shirt out flat, measure and mark 4 (4½, 5, 5½)" down from each underarm seam, and follow the cutting instructions on page 6. Mark the center front and center back.

2. Position and press the seashell appliqué onto the center front of the T-shirt and follow the product instructions for pressing time.

3. Press the puff sleeves flat. Along the pressed fold, cut a slit opening from the shoulder to the sleeve hem band. Do not cut through the double-thick hem band. Cut a 2" length of sequin trim. Pull the trim through the cut opening and wrap around the hem band. Handstitch the trim to form a loop. Position and tack the sewn trim seam inside the T-shirt. Repeat for the second sleeve.

SEWING THE SKIRT

4. Measure the circumference of the T-shirt at the chest and multiply by 1½ to determine the dotted metallic stretch fabric cutting width. Use the chart below to cut the skirt length.

	S (2/3)	M (4/5)	L (6/6x)	XL (7/8)
Skirt length	20"	22"	24"	28"

5. Finish-stitch the top long side of the fabric for a waistline edge. With right sides facing, fold and sew the short sides to make the skirt back seam. Fold to divide the skirt into quarters and mark the sides and front.

6. On the waistline edge, sew two rows of basting stitches for gathering; sew one row ¼" from the edge and the second row ¼" below that.

7. Lay the skirt piece flat with the sewn seam centered in the back. Mark the front centerline. Along the side edges, measure and mark 7" up from the cut hem. Cut an angle from each side edge mark to the front and back center marks. Finish-stitch the edges.

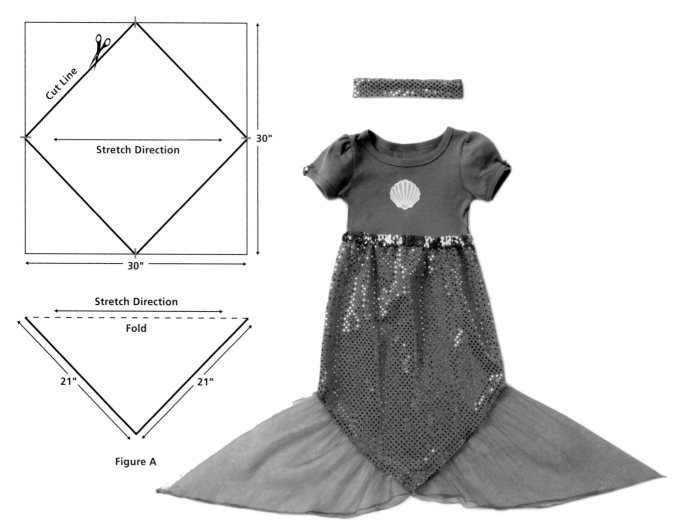

Figure A

MAKING THE FINS

8. The glitter tulle used in the sample is stretchy, so special cutting instructions are needed for the draping of this fabric. If your fabric does not stretch, cut two pieces of fabric 21"x 21".

9. If your tulle does stretch, cut two 30" squares of the stretchy tulle. Fold and mark the center of all four sides. Refer to Figure A and cut an angle connecting each mark to form a 21" square with the stretch direction running across the center.

10. With wrong sides together, fold and press each 21" square fabric in half to form a triangle. Sew the cut edges together ¼" from the edge. Fold and press the cut edges over and zigzag-stitch along the fabric edge to form a narrow hem. Trim away any excess hem allowance.

11. On the fold edge, sew two rows of basting stitches for gathering; sew one row ¼" from the edge and the second row ¼" below that. Fold the fabric to mark the center of the gathered edge. Evenly distribute the gathers. With right sides together, match the center of the fin to the side edge of the skirt. Sew the fin to the skirt, starting at the skirt side edge toward the skirt point. Topstitch along the seam to keep the hem lying flat. Repeat for the second fin. Remove all the gathering stitches.

31

Under the Sea

ATTACHING THE SKIRT TO THE WAISTBAND

12. Pull the basting threads to gather the skirt waistline. With right sides together, sew the skirt to the T-shirt, using a narrow zigzag stitch and matching the side, front, and back marks. Remove all the gathering stitches.

13. Measure the circumference of the T-shirt at the chest to determine the cutting length of the sequin trim. Starting at the back, handstitch the sequin trim around the waistline, covering the seam.

MAKING THE HEADBAND

14. Measure the circumference of the child's head to determine the cutting width of the dotted metallic stretch fabric. Cut the length at 5". With right sides together, fold the fabric in half and sew the long edges together to create a tube. Turn the tube right side out and turn in one end. Tuck the other end inside the tube and handstitch the ends together. ■

In this FIERCE
costume,
she can save
HERSELF from
any dangers.

Little Red

Little Red

She's off to Grandmother's house, where you always get the best treats. Just remind her to watch out for the Big Bad Wolf! A laced bodice, eyelet trim, and a dramatic red hood are straight out of a fairy tale.

Instructions are for sizes Small (Medium, Large, Extra-Large). Select the size to sew based on the closest matching chest measurement in the chart on page 6. All seam allowances are ½" unless otherwise noted.

WHAT YOU'LL NEED

• Basic tool kit (see page 7)

• T-shirt: white, long sleeve

• Red quilt cotton (see yardage chart at right)

• ¾ yard 44"-wide black quilt cotton

• ½ yard 44"-wide white eyelet-border batiste fabric

• 2"-wide white cotton ruffled eyelet lace trim (see yardage chart at right)

• 2 yards ⅜" dark red grosgrain ribbon

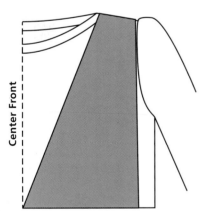

Figure A

44"-wide fabric	S (2/3)	M (4/5)	L (6/6x)	XL (7/8)
Red cotton	2 yards	2¼ yards	2½ yards	2¾ yards

2"-wide trim	S (2/3)	M (4/5)	L (6/6x)	XL (7/8)
Eyelet lace	2½ yards	2¾ yards	3 yards	3¼ yards

PREPARING THE T-SHIRT

1. Lay the T-shirt out flat, measure and mark 3 (3½, 4, 4½)" down from each underarm seam, and follow the cutting instructions on page 6. Mark the center front and center back.

SEWING THE BODICE

2. To determine the cutting dimensions of the black fabric for the vest bodice, refer to Figure A. Lay the T-shirt out flat and align the edge of a piece of plain paper down the T-shirt sleeve edge. Trim the paper width at the T-shirt center front. Feeling with your fingers through the paper, trace the angle of the shoulder seam. Draw a line from the shoulder inside edge to the waistline center mark. Cut out the paper template. With two fabric layers, right sides together, trace the vest shape onto the black fabric, twice. Sew directly on the marking lines. Do not sew across the bottom edge. Trim ¼" from the sewn edges. Clip the corners and turn them right side out. Press flat and topstitch the three edges.

3. Lay the vest pieces flat, reflecting both sides. Sew the eyelet trim ¼" from the inside edges. Handstitch the vest piece to the shoulder seam, turning under the rough trim edges. Baste-stitch the vest pieces to the T-shirt waistline. Cut and arrange the ribbon in a crisscross pattern, as seen in the photo. Handstitch into place.

4. To make the waistband belt, cut a length of the black fabric at 6". Measure the circumference of the T-shirt at the chest and add 2" to determine the fabric cutting width. Sew the short edges right sides together to create a circle. Fold in half, with wrong sides together, to create a double-thick 3" waistband. Baste-stitch and finish the edge. Fold the waistband into quarters and mark the sides, front, and back center. Matching marks, sew the waistband to the T-shirt using a narrow zigzag stitch.

5. Cut 2" off the sleeve cuffs. Stretching the fabric slightly, sew the eyelet trim around the edge. Turn under and sew the rough trim edges.

SEWING THE APRON

6. For a double-thickness apron, cut two pieces of batiste fabric according to the chart below. With one layer of fabric, sew the red ribbon 1½" from the bottom edge. With the fabric pieces right sides together, sew around three sides, leaving the top open. Clip the corners and turn right side out. Press and topstitch along the side edges. Sew the 2" eyelet trim to the hem edge. Press flat and edgestitch along the seam to keep it lying flat. Finish-stitch the top edge of the apron.

	S (2/3)	M (4/5)	L (6/6x)	XL (7/8)
Apron dimensions	12" x 12"	13" x 13"	14" x 14"	15" x 15"

Little Red

SEWING THE SKIRT

7. To determine the skirt fabric cutting width, measure the circumference of the T-shirt at the chest and multiply by 2. If the width measurement is wider than the fabric width, divide that number in half. Then cut two red cotton fabric pieces and sew them together. This creates two side seams and prevents an awkward seam placement. Use the chart below to cut the skirt length.

	S (2/3)	M (4/5)	L (6/6x)	XL (7/8)
Skirt length	14"	15"	16"	18"

8. Finish-stitch along the top and bottom edges. With right sides facing, fold and sew the sides to make the back seam of the skirt. Sew the ruffle trim to the hem edge. Press flat and edgestitch along the seam to keep it lying flat. On the finished waistline edge, fold into quarters and mark the sides, front, and back center. Center and baste the apron on top of the skirt. Sew two rows of basting stitches for gathering; sew one row ¼" from the edge and the second row ¼" below that.

ATTACHING THE SKIRT TO THE T-SHIRT

9. Pull the threads to gather the skirt waistline. With right sides together, matching the marks, sew the skirt to the waistband. Remove all the gathering stitches.

SEWING THE HOODED CAPE

10. To determine the cutting dimensions of the red fabric for the hood, refer to the chart below. Cut four fabric layers.

	S (2/3)	M (4/5)	L (6/6x)	XL (7/8)
Hood dimensions	10" x 12"	10" x 12"	12" x 14"	12" x 14"

11. Mark and cut a rounded corner as in Figure B. Transfer that corner curve and cut all four layers the same. Pin two fabric pieces with right sides together. Sew the rounded corner and two edges to create the back of the hood. Repeat this with the other two fabric pieces. Clip the curved seam allowance and press flat. Nest and pin the two hood pieces with right sides together and sew along the front hood edge. Turn the hood right side out. Press and topstitch along the front of the hood. Baste-stitch the bottom of the hood closed.

12. To create the neckband, cut the red fabric length at 3". Cut the width according to the chart below.

	S (2/3)	M (4/5)	L (6/6x)	XL (7/8)
Neck band width	44"	44"	52"	52"

13. Fold the strip lengthwise with right sides together and press. Sew a ¼" seam along the three open edges. Leave a section open enough to tuck in the bottom of the hood. Clip the corners and turn right side out. Mark the center of the neckband. Measure the circumference of the child's neck, then add 2". Take that measurement and center those marks on the neckband. Pin the hood center within the edge opening of the neckband. Pin the corner edges of the hood to the neck measurement marks. Fold a pleat in the center back of the hood to flatten out the fabric to the edge. Baste the hood in place. Press and topstitch along all edges, closing the hood within the neckband.

14. To create the cape, keep the red fabric width of 44". To determine the fabric cutting length, measure from the dress shoulder to the hem, then add 2". As in Figure C, mark along the top edge of the fabric 10" from each side. Cut from that mark to the corner to create a trapezoid shape. Draw a 10" circle paper template. Align at the bottom points and cut to round the corners. Sew a narrow hem (see page 10) on all cut edges.

15. Along the top of the cape, fold the edge over and sew a 1" hem. On the wrong side of the neckband (i.e., inside of the hood), pin the cape center to the neckband center mark. Pin the corner edges of the cape to the neck measurement marks. Fold two pleats on each side of the center mark. Flatten the pleated fabric toward the edges. Press and sew along the top and bottom edges of the neckband. ■

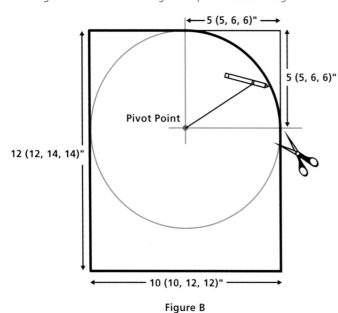

Figure B

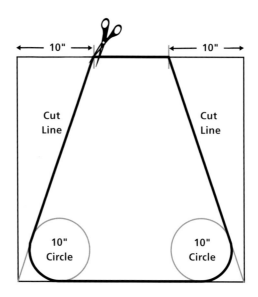

Figure C

If you don't
have
PIXIE DUST,
fill the
satchel with
CANDY.

Fairy Tale

Fairy Tale

This whimsical fairy will flutter and fly through the party. Embellished organza creates beautiful wings that are surprisingly sturdy but light.

Instructions are for sizes Small (Medium, Large, Extra-Large). Select the size to sew based on the closest matching chest measurement in the chart on page 6. All seam allowances are ½" unless otherwise noted.

WHAT YOU'LL NEED
- Basic tool kit (see page 7)
- String and marking pen
- T-shirt: green, long sleeve

For the skirt:
- Green quilt cotton (see yardage chart at right)
- Petal skirt template (page 128)

For the wings:
- Embellished yellow organza (see yardage chart at right)
- ½ yard ⅜"-wide yellow-gold single-faced satin ribbon
- Liquid seam sealant

For the waist and neck trim:
- 1⅞"-wide satin ruffled blanket binding (see yardage chart at right)

For the satchel:
- 5" x 10" green glitter felt sheet
- 1 yard ⅝"-wide green grosgrain ribbon
- 1 hook-and-loop dot

	S (2/3)	M (4/5)	L (6/6x)	XL (7/8)
44"-wide quilt cotton	1¼ yards	1¼ yards	1½ yards	2¼ yards
58"-wide organza	1½ yards	1¾ yards	1¾ yards	2¼ yards
Satin ruffle	1¼ yards	1½ yards	1½ yards	1½ yards

PREPARING THE T-SHIRT

1. Lay the T-shirt out flat, measure and mark 4 (4½, 5, 5½)" down from each underarm seam, and follow the cutting instructions on page 6. Mark the center front and center back.

2. Measure the circumference of the neckline and add 1" to determine the length to cut the satin ruffle trim. Starting at the back of the neck, using a narrow zigzag stitch, sew the trim ¼" from the edge of the T-shirt neckline. Overlap and turn under the trim ends. Avoid stretching the neckline as you sew.

SEWING THE SKIRT

3. Make 7 (7, 8, 9) skirt petals: For each petal, cut two cotton fabric pieces 5" wide by the skirt length in the chart below.

	S (2/3)	M (4/5)	L (6/6x)	XL (7/8)
Skirt length	13"	14"	15"	17"

4. Copy the petal skirt template. Place two pieces of fabric right sides together. Place the petal skirt template centered at one end of the double fabric piece. Trace and cut out the petal point. Sew a ½" seam along the sides to the point. Clip and turn right side out and press flat. Repeat for all of the petals.

5. Measure the circumference of the T-shirt at the chest and add 2" to determine the cotton fabric cutting width. Use the chart below to cut the length for the underskirt.

	S (2/3)	M (4/5)	L (6/6x)	XL (7/8)
Underskirt length	8½"	9"	9½"	11"

6. Finish-stitch all the edges. Sew a narrow hem (see page 10) on one side. On the waistline edge, sew two rows of basting stitches for gathering; sew one row ¼" from the edge and the second row ¼" below that. Fold to divide the skirt into quarters and mark the sides and front. Lay flat to attach the petals.

7. Arrange and sew the petals along the underskirt waistline edge. Evenly space and overlap the petals, allowing ½" on both edges for a back seam. Sew the petals to the underskirt. Sew the short edges right sides together to create the back seam. Fold to divide the waistband into quarters and mark the sides and front. Sew the ruffle trim to the finished edge of the waistband.

TIP
Cut out a template on scrap cotton fabric, then pin it to the organza before cutting.

ATTACHING THE SKIRT TO THE T-SHIRT

8. With right sides together, sew the skirt to the T-shirt, making sure to catch the petal edges and ruffle within the seam. Use a narrow zigzag stitch, matching sides, front, and back marks.

CREATING THE WINGS

9. Cut two pieces of organza fabric the measurement along both T-shirt sleeves and the back of the neck, then add 2". To determine the fabric cutting length, measure the finished dress length and add 2".

10. Create a sturdy ½" French seam (see page 9) along the top edge. With the seam edge at top, fold the fabric in half. As in Figure A, mark the sides to determine a bottom square area. The fold-edge mark becomes the pivot point for marking an overall quarter circle edge. Use a string attached to a marking pen to draw the curved edge. Make a 6" circle paper template. Starting at the fold edge, mark tangent circles along the quarter circle edge until the last circle meets the side cut edge. Using sharp scissors, cut a scalloped edge and run a bead of seam sealant along the edge. Both fabric layers will be bonded together.

11. Cut two 12" strips of yellow satin ribbon. Fold one into a loop and handstitch it to the top edge at the tip of the wing. Repeat for the other tip of the wing. Handstitch the center of the wings to the center back neck of the T-shirt.

CREATING THE PIXIE DUST SATCHEL

12. Cut a 5" x 10" rectangle of glitter felt. Cut rounded corners at the top of the 5" edge. Fold the bottom edge up to create a 5" x 4" pouch. Sew the two 4" side edges. Fold the top over and press the edge to create a satchel front flap. Handstitch the hook-and-loop dot for the closure. Cut the green grosgrain ribbon to a desired crossover strap length. Sew the ribbon to the back of the satchel. ■

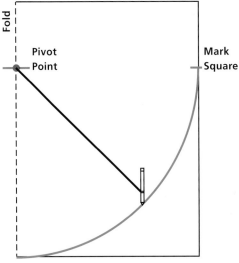

Fold

Pivot Point

Mark Square

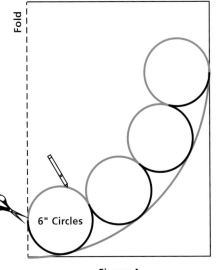

Fold

6" Circles

Figure A

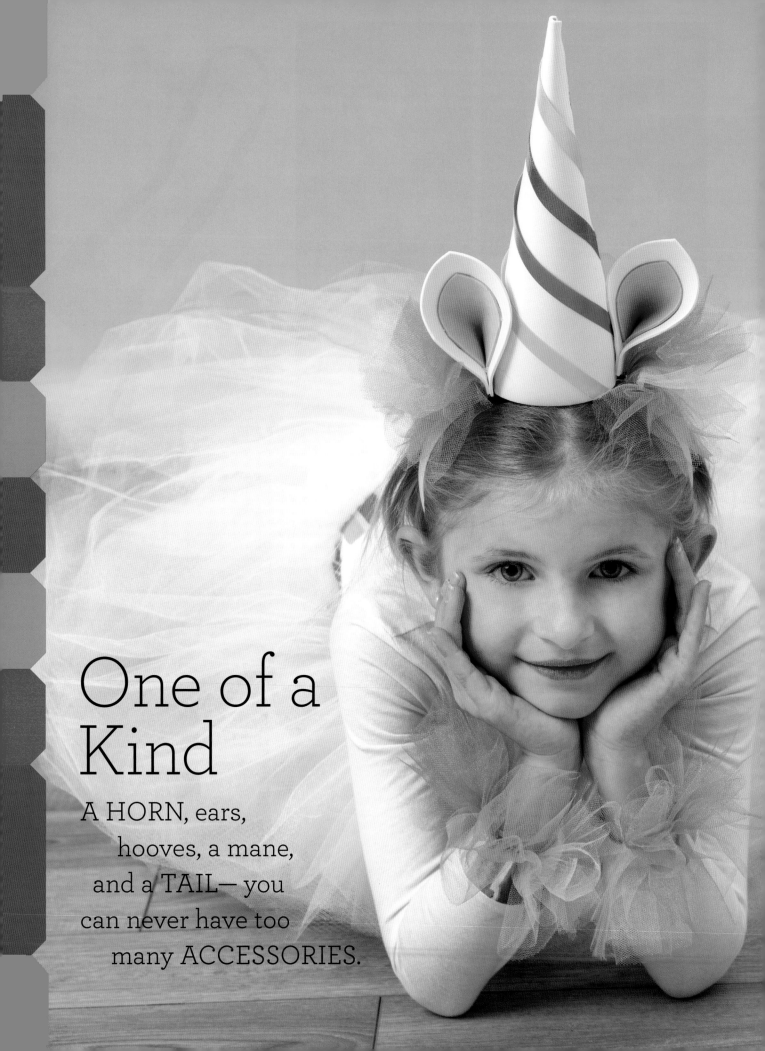

One of a Kind

A HORN, ears, hooves, a mane, and a TAIL— you can never have too many ACCESSORIES.

One of a Kind

It's common knowledge that no two unicorns look exactly alike. Use any and every color of tulle you want to make your little unicorn's costume as unique as she is.

Instructions are for sizes Small (Medium, Large, Extra-Large). Select the size to sew based on the closest matching chest measurement in the chart on page 6. All seam allowances are ½" unless otherwise noted.

WHAT YOU'LL NEED
- Basic tool kit (see page 7)

- Bias-tape maker (optional)

- Hot-glue gun and glue sticks

- T-shirt: white, long sleeve

- 4 sew-in hook-and-loop dots

For bodice, cuffs, and accessories:
- ½ yard 44"-wide rainbow-stripe quilt cotton

For the bodice and underskirt:
- White quilt cotton (see yardage chart at right)

For the skirt:
- White tulle and white nylon netting (see yardage chart at right)

For the mane, tail, and accessories:
- One 6" x 5 yard roll each of pink, turquoise, yellow, and citrus green shiny tulle

For the horn/ears:
- Horn template (page 129)

- Unicorn ears template (page 128)

- 1 each 9" x 12" white and pink 2mm foam sheets

- Rubber bands

- Single-faced ⅜"-wide satin ribbon: ¼ yard each yellow, pink, and turquoise

- ¼" paper punch

- 2 white pipe cleaners

- White ¾" headband

44"-wide fabric	S (2/3)	M (4/5)	L (6/6x)	XL (7/8)
White cotton	½ yard	¾ yard	¾ yard	¾ yard

54"-wide fabric	S (2/3)	M (4/5)	L (6/6x)	XL (7/8)
White tulle	3¾ yards	4 yards	4¼ yards	4½ yards
Nylon netting	2 yards	2 yards	2¼ yards	2¼ yards

PREPARING THE T-SHIRT
1. Lay the T-shirt out flat, measure and mark 1½ (2, 2½, 3)" down from each underarm seam, and follow the cutting instructions on page 6. Mark the center front and center back.

SEWING THE BODICE
2. To make a striped T-shirt bodice, measure the circumference of the T-shirt at the chest and add 2" to determine the fabric cutting width. Cut two rainbow fabric strips at 2", one white fabric strip at 2", and one at 4" for the cutting length.

3. Using ½" seams, with right sides together, sew rainbow strips to either long edge of the 2" white fabric strip. (To make the stripe widths match, use a bias-tape maker.) Turn under and press ½" edges of the rainbow fabric. With right sides up, center the rainbow piece over the 4" white fabric piece, leaving a ½" white fabric edge top and bottom. Topstitch the rainbow fabric piece to the white backing fabric. With right sides together, sew the short edges to create the back seam. Fold the piece to divide it into quarters and mark the sides, front, and back.

4. With right sides together, using a narrow zigzag stitch, sew the bodice to the cut T-shirt waistline as close to the top rainbow stripe as possible.

MAKING THE MANE
5. Cut one piece of each color tulle 6" wide by the length in the chart below. Stack and pin the strips of tulle and sew two rows of basting stitches ¼" apart, down the center length. Pull the basting threads to gather. Using a narrow zigzag stitch, sew the tulle to the center back of the T-shirt. Fold the tulle edges over and press to one side. Sew the layers together close to the seam but not catching the T-shirt. Remove any visible gathering threads. Separate and fluff layers.

	S (2/3)	M (4/5)	L (6/6x)	XL (7/8)
Tulle length	37"	39"	21"	25"

SEWING THE SKIRT
6. Measure the circumference of the T-shirt at the chest and multiply by 1½ to determine the white cotton fabric cutting width. Refer to the chart below for the underskirt cutting length.

	S (2/3)	M (4/5)	L (6/6x)	XL (7/8)
Underskirt length	10"	11"	12"	13"

One of a Kind

7. Finish-stitch along the top and bottom edges. With right sides facing, sew and finish-stitch the sides to make the back seam of the skirt. On the waistline edge, sew two rows of basting stitches for gathering: sew one row ¼" from the edge and the second row ¼" below that. Fold to divide the skirt into quarters and mark the sides, and front. Create a narrow hem (see page 10) on the bottom edge.

8. To make two tulle pieces and one netting piece, measure the circumference of the T-shirt at the chest and multiply by 3 to determine the fabric cutting length. Fold each piece of tulle and netting lengthwise, twice to create four fabric layers. Sew two rows of basting stitches for gathering: sew one row ¼" from the folded edge and the second row ¼" below that. Cut the width in the chart below, measuring from the basting seam. Fold each piece to divide into quarters and mark the center and side seams.

	S (2/3)	M (4/5)	L (6/6x)	XL (7/8)
Tulle/nylon width	10"	11"	12"	13"

9. Pull the basting threads to gather. Pin and match the sides and center markings. Starting at the back, sew one tulle piece flat to the underskirt below the double-baste stitching on the underskirt edge. To alternate the open short edges between the pieces, start at the side seam and sew the second piece of tulle beneath the first tulle piece. Start at the other side seam to sew the netting piece beneath both tulle pieces. Fluff and separate the layers for fullness.

ATTACHING THE SKIRT TO THE T-SHIRT
10. Pull the basting threads to gather the underskirt waistline. With right sides together, sew the skirt to the T-shirt, making sure to catch the top layer of tulle within the seam; use a narrow zigzag stitch, matching sides, front, and back marks. Remove all gathering stitches.

MAKING THE TAIL
11. Cut one piece of each color tulle 6" wide by the length in the chart below. Cut each piece into 3"-wide strips and stack together. On the short end, fold the edge over ½" and sew all layers together. Handstitch the tail to the back of the T-shirt at the waistline, below the mane.

	S (2/3)	M (4/5)	L (6/6x)	XL (7/8)
Tail length	18"	20"	22"	26"

MAKING THE ACCESSORIES
12. To make unicorn hooves, measure the ankle and wrist circumferences. Cut two rainbow fabric strips 4½" wide by the wrist measurement plus 3". Then cut two more rainbow fabric strips 4½" wide by the ankle measurement plus 3". Fold each piece of fabric in half lengthwise. As in Figure A, sew across the short ends and 1" of the length on each side. Turn the piece right side out and press flat to create a strap.

13. Cut one piece of each color tulle 6" wide by twice the finished strap measurement. Hand-gather, then fold in half widthwise to create a 3" double-layered tuft. Baste across the fold. Repeat for the other three colors. Tuck and pin each tuft into the open edge of the strap. Closing the opening, topstitch all the edges. Hand-sew hook-and-loop dots to the 1" ends. Repeat step 13 for all four hooves.

Fold

Figure A

14. For the wrist "hooves," cut 2" off the T-shirt cuffs. With right sides together, using a narrow zigzag stitch, sew the straps to the T-shirt sleeves, leaving a 1" end free to overlap and close with hook-and-loop dot.

15. To make the unicorn horn, copy and tape the template to the white foam sheet. Cut out the shape with a sharp craft knife. Glue along the indicated edge, using rubber bands to help hold the foam cone into shape. When the glue is dry, hot-glue colored ribbons in place to spiral around the cone. Punch two side holes near the base of the horn.

16. To make the unicorn ears, trim the template to the outer ear lines and tape to the white foam sheet. Cut out two with a sharp craft knife. Trim the template to the center ear lines and tape to the pink foam sheet. Cut out two with a sharp craft knife. Hot-glue the pink piece to the center of the white ear piece. Pinch the bottom edges of each ear and glue together. Glue the ears to each side of the horn above the punched holes. Wrap a pipe cleaner around the headband and through the horn's punched holes to secure in place. Cut the 6"-wide tulle to 6" lengths in each color. Hand-gather, then fold in half widthwise to create a 3"-wide double-layered tuft. Baste across the fold. Repeat for all the colors. Hot-glue the tufts in place to hide the pipe cleaners. ■

47

Celebrate!

Now she
can have
her CAKE
and
WEAR IT,
too!

Celebrate!

Everyone will know who the birthday girl is when she dons this sweet ensemble. Adjust the size of the candles to match the number to her age.

Instructions are for sizes Small (Medium, Large, Extra-Large). Select the size to sew based on the closest matching chest measurement in the chart on page 6. All seam allowances are ½" unless otherwise noted.

WHAT YOU'LL NEED
- Basic tool kit (see page 7)
- Craft knife
- Hot-glue gun and glue sticks
- T-shirt: white, sleeveless
- Birthday candle template (page 130)
- Yellow, turquoise, and pink 5" x 5" iron-on twill patches

For the skirt:
- Turquoise polka-dot quilt cotton (see yardage chart at right)
- Yellow and pink polka-dot quilt cotton (see yardage chart at right)
- 33 (33, 36, 39) turquoise, yellow, and pink buttons
- Turquoise, pink, and yellow single-faced satin ribbon (see yardage chart at right)
- White double-faced satin ribbon (see yardage chart at right)

For the accessories:
- Pink ½"-wide headband
- ½ yard ¾" white elastic
- 25 small buttons in multiple colors

44"-wide fabric	S (2/3)	M (4/5)	L (6/6x)	XL (7/8)
Turquoise quilt cotton	1¼ yards	1¼ yards	1½ yards	1½ yards
Pink and yellow quilt cotton	¾ yard	¾ yard	1 yard	1 yard

⅜-wide satin ribbon	S (2/3)	M (4/5)	L (6/6x)	XL (7/8)
Turquoise, pink, and yellow	2 yards	2¼ yards	2½ yards	2¾ yards
White	6 yards	6¾ yards	7½ yards	8¼ yards

PREPARING THE T-SHIRT

1. Lay the T-shirt out flat, measure and mark 3½ (4, 4½, 4½)" down from each underarm seam, and follow the cutting instructions on page 6. Mark the center front and center back.

2. Copy the birthday candle template and lightly tape over the iron-on twill patches. With a sharp craft blade, carefully cut out each candle shape. Center and evenly space the candles along the front of the T-shirt. Repeat with the yellow flame shape and follow product instructions for pressing time. (Reduce the template size to create additional candles.)

SEWING THE SKIRT

3. Measure the circumference of the T-shirt at the chest and multiply times 1½ to determine the desired cutting width of the underskirt. Referring to the chart below for the cutting length, cut the underskirt from the turquoise fabric.

	S (2/3)	M (4/5)	L (6/6x)	XL (7/8)
Underskirt length	10"	11"	13"	14"

4. Finish-stitch all the edges. On the waistline edge, sew two rows of basting stitches for gathering: sew one row ¼" from the edge and the second row ¼" below that.

5. Fold to divide the skirt into quarters and mark the sides and front center seam. Lay the underskirt flat to attach the ruffles.

6. To make three ruffles, measure the circumference of the T-shirt at the chest and multiply times 2½ to determine the fabric cutting width. With turquoise, yellow, and pink polka-dot fabric, cut the length to the measurement in the chart below.

	S (2/3)	M (4/5)	L (6/6x)	XL (7/8)
Ruffle length	10"	11"	13"	14"

7. Cut and sew together extra strips to obtain the total width. With wrong sides facing, fold each ruffle in half lengthwise and press to create a double-thickness ruffle. Baste and finish-stitch the cut edges. Sew two rows of basting stitches for gathering; sew one row ¼" from the edge and the second row ¼" below that. Fold each ruffle into quarters and mark the sides and front center seam.

8. For all three ruffles, follow the ribbon and fabric color order in the photo. Mark along the folded edge every 5". With pins, mark each ribbon every 6". Align pins and fabric marks, then tack ribbon to the edge of the ruffle to create ribbon scallops. Adjust measurements near the outer edges (back seam) to even out spacing.

9. To attach the ruffles to the underskirt, start with the turquoise bottom ruffle and pull the gathering threads and arrange evenly. With right sides together, match marks and sew to the bottom edge of the underskirt. With the pink top ruffle, pull the gathering threads and arrange evenly. With right sides out, match the marks and pin to the waistband of the underskirt. Sew just below the gathering stitches on the underskirt. Mark the bottom edge of the top ruffle onto the underskirt. With the yellow middle ruffle, pull the gathering threads and arrange evenly. Position and sew to the underskirt, about 1½" above the marked ruffle edge. With right sides together, sew the side edges of the skirt together to create the back seam. Hand-sew buttons where the ribbon scallops are tacked to the skirt.

ATTACHING THE SKIRT TO THE T-SHIRT

10. Pull the basting threads to gather the skirt waistline. With right sides together (see TIP), sew the skirt to the T-shirt, making sure to catch the ruffle sewn edge within the seam; use a narrow zigzag stitch, matching sides, front, and back marks. Remove all the gathering threads.

MAKING THE BUTTON BRACELET AND HEADBAND

11. Cut the elastic to a comfortable length to fit the wrist and add 1" for seam overlap. Measure the child's wrist circumference and multiply by 2. Cut the fabric to that length measurement and the width at 2".

12. With right sides together, fold in half and sew along the long edge to create a tube. Turn right side out. Pull the elastic through the tube and sew the ends of the elastic together. Turn under one edge of the tube. Tuck the other end inside the tube and handstitch together. Hand-sew buttons to decorate, taking care not to sew through the elastic.

13. Hot-glue buttons to the purchased headband. ■

TIP
To help handle the bulkiness when sewing the skirt to the T-shirt, turn the skirt inside out and place the T-shirt inside the skirt.

51

With her
SHERIFF'S
badge, she'll
CLEAN UP
the town and
her toys.
Wild West

Wild West

There's a new sheriff in town, and she's taking control in style! The attached microsuede half-vest looks authentic enough for official duty.

Instructions are for sizes Small (Medium, Large, Extra-Large). Select the size to sew based on the closest matching chest measurement in the chart on page 6. All seam allowances are ½" unless otherwise noted.

WHAT YOU'LL NEED

- Basic tool kit (see page 7)

- Craft knife

- T-shirt: white, long sleeve

- 3–5 white shirt buttons

- Black polyester fringe (see yardage chart at right)

For the skirt:
- ½ yard 44"-wide bandana patchwork print cotton calico

For the vest:
- Black microsuede fabric (see yardage chart at right)

For the badge:
- Metallic gold iron-on transfer sheet

- Sheriff star template (page 130)

58"-wide fabric	S (2/3)	M (4/5)	L (6/6x)	XL (7/8)
Microsuede	½ yard	½ yard	¾ yard	¾ yard

2"-wide fringe	S (2/3)	M (4/5)	L (6/6x)	XL (7/8)
Black polyester	1¾ yards	1¾ yards	2 yards	2 yards

PREPARING THE T-SHIRT
1. Lay the T-shirt out flat, measure and mark 4 (4½, 5, 5½)" down from each underarm seam, and follow the cutting instructions on page 6. Mark at the center front and center back.

SEWING THE VEST
2. To determine the cutting dimensions for the microsuede vest fabric, measure the T-shirt length from the shoulder to the cut waistline. Refer to the chart below for the fabric cutting width. Cut two.

	S (2/3)	M (4/5)	L (6/6x)	XL (7/8)
Vest cutting width	24"	25"	27"	29"

3. Lay the T-shirt out flat, align the edge of a piece of plain paper down the shirt front center, and trim the paper width at the side seam. Feeling with your fingers through the paper, trace the approximate armhole curve, base of the neckline, and shoulder seam. Mark as in Figure A. Cut out the paper template. With two fabric layers, right sides together, trace the vest shape onto the microsuede fabric, twice. Sew directly on the marking lines. Do not sew across the bottom edge. Trim ¼" from the sewn edges, clip the curved seam allowances, turn right side out, and press. Topstitch all the edges, turning under and closing the bottom edge.

4. Lay the vest pieces flat, reflecting both sides. Sew the fringe trim straight across from the armpit seam, as shown on Figure A.

TIP
You don't need to draw perfectly smooth curved lines when creating the template. Once sewn as a seam line, imperfections in the line will smooth out in the fabric.

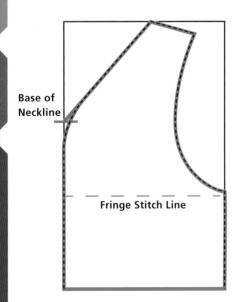

Base of Neckline

Fringe Stitch Line

Figure A

5. Copy the sheriff star template and lightly tape it over the iron-on transfer sheet. With a sharp craft knife, carefully cut out the shape. Place the star above the fringe on the vest and follow the product instructions for pressing time.

6. Handstitch the vest pieces to the shoulder and side seams. Evenly space and sew buttons down the center front of the T-shirt.

SEWING THE WAISTBAND

7. Measure the circumference of the T-shirt at the chest and add 2" to determine the fabric cutting width. Cut the black microsuede fabric by 5" length to create a waistband. Sew the short edges right sides together to create the back seam. Fold in half lengthwise, with wrong sides together, to create a double-thick waistband. Baste-stitch and finish the edge. Fold into quarter segments and mark the sides, front, and back center. Use a narrow zigzag stitch and matching sides, front, and back marks, sew the waistband to the T-shirt.

SEWING THE SKIRT

8. Measure the circumference of the T-shirt at the chest and multiply by 1½ to determine the patchwork skirt fabric cutting width. Use the chart below to cut the length for the skirt.

	S (2/3)	M (4/5)	L (6/6x)	XL (7/8)
Skirt length	11"	12"	13"	15"

9. Finish-stitch along the top and bottom edges. With right sides facing, fold and sew the sides to create the back seam of the skirt. On the waistline edge, sew two rows of basting stitches for gathering; sew one row ¼" from the edge and the second row ¼" below that. Fold to divide the skirt into quarters and mark the sides, front, and back. With right sides together, sew the fringe to the bottom edge of the skirt. Press flat and edgestitch along the fringe seam to keep it lying flat.

ATTACHING THE SKIRT TO THE T-SHIRT

10. Pull the threads to gather the skirt waistline. With right sides together and matching marks, sew the skirt to the T-shirt waistband. Remove all gathering stitches. ■

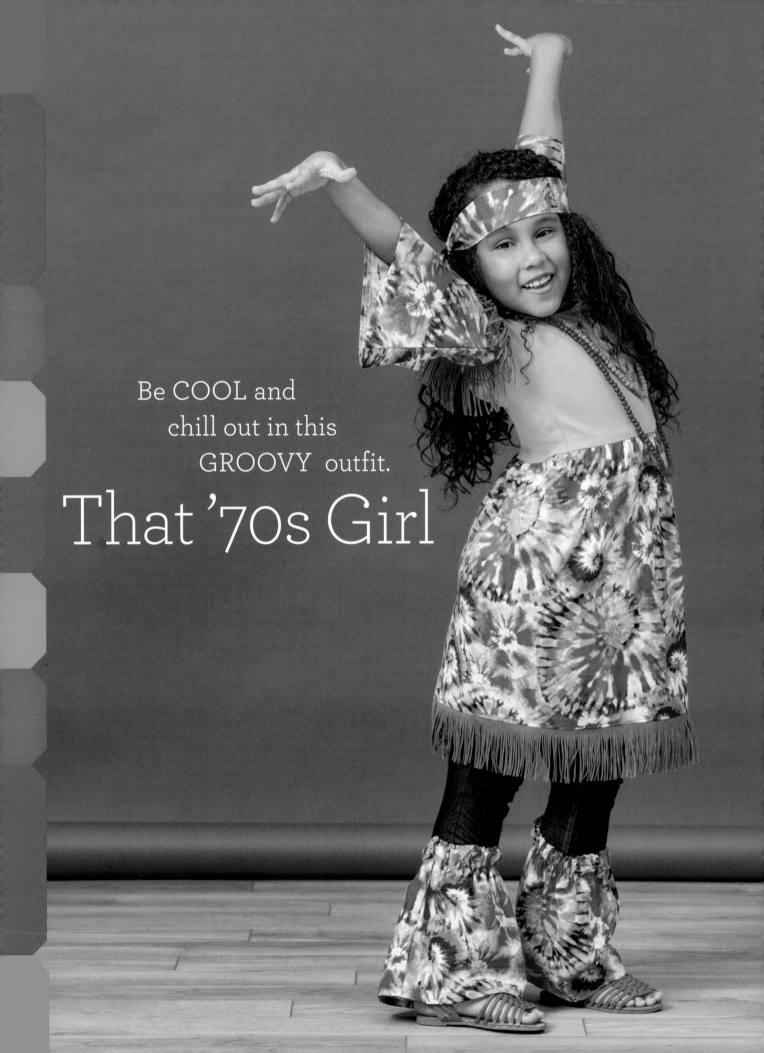

Be COOL and
chill out in this
GROOVY outfit.

That '70s Girl

That '70s Girl

This is the dawning of the age of bell-bottoms, fringe, and psychedelic colors. An appliqué peace symbol completes the classic hippie look.

Instructions are for sizes Small (Medium, Large, Extra-Large). Select the size to sew based on the closest matching chest measurement in the chart on page 6. All seam allowances are ½" unless otherwise noted.

WHAT YOU'LL NEED
• Basic tool kit (see page 7)

• Craft knife

• T-shirt: aqua, short sleeve

For the skirt, sleeve, and bell-bottom extensions:
• Tie-dye calico-print cotton (see yardage chart at right)

• 3" brown woven fringe trim

For the bell-bottom leggings:
• ½ yard 1" white elastic

For the peace sign appliqué:
• Double-sided fusible web

• Peace sign template (page 130)

44"-wide fabric	S (2/3)	M (4/5)	L (6/6x)	XL (7/8)
Cotton tie-dye print	1¼ yards	1¼ yards	1¼ yards	1½ yards
3"-wide trim	**S (2/3)**	**M (4/5)**	**L (6/6x)**	**XL (7/8)**
Fringe	1¾ yards	1¾ yards	2 yards	2 yards

PREPARING THE T-SHIRT
1. Lay the T-shirt out flat, measure and mark 4 (4½, 5, 5½)" down from each underarm seam, and follow the cutting instructions on page 6. Mark the center front and center back.

2. Cut a 6" square piece of tie-dye fabric and a 6" square piece of double fusible web. Follow the product instructions for pressing time and correct side to use, then fuse the web to the wrong side of the fabric. Copy and cut out the peace sign template and lightly tape it over the fusible web. With a sharp craft knife, carefully cut out the shape. Peel off the fusible web paper. Place the cutout onto the center front of the T-shirt and press in place.

SEWING THE SLEEVE EXTENSIONS
3. Cut off the existing hem of the T-shirt sleeves. Cut two pieces of tie-dye fabric according to Figure A to create the sleeve extensions. To determine the cutting dimensions, measure the circumference of the T-shirt sleeve opening, then add 1". That is Measurement A. Double that total to determine cutting Measurement B. Measure the length between the child's armpit to the wrist. Subtract the length of the existing sleeve from the armpit to the T-shirt edge. Then add 1" to that total to arrive at cutting Measurement C. Cut the fabric from the bottom corners to the top measurement marks.

4. Finish the top and bottom edges. Sew the fringe trim to the fabric right side, top edge. With right sides together, sew the angled side seams of the sleeves together and finish-stitch the edge. Sew a narrow hem (see page 10) on the bottom edge. Fold to divide the sleeve extension and T-shirt sleeve into quarters to mark the bottom (side seam), top, front, and back. With right sides together, using a narrow zigzag stitch and matching marks, sew the sleeve extension to the sleeve.

SEWING THE SKIRT
5. Measure the circumference of the T-shirt at the chest and multiply by 1½ to determine the skirt fabric cutting width. Use the chart measurements below to cut the skirt length.

	S (2/3)	M (4/5)	L (6/6x)	XL (7/8)
Skirt length	11"	12"	13"	14"

6. Finish-stitch along the top and bottom edges. With right sides together, sew and finish-stitch the side edges to create a back seam. On the waistline edge, sew two rows of basting stitches for gathering: sew one row ¼" from the edge and the second row ¼" below that. Fold the skirt into quarters and mark the sides, front, and back center. With right sides together, sew the fringe to the bottom edge of the skirt. Press flat and edgestitch along the fringe seam to keep it lying flat.

ATTACHING THE SKIRT TO THE T-SHIRT

7. Pull the threads to gather the skirt waistline. With right sides together, and using a narrow zigzag stitch and matching marks, sew the skirt to the T-shirt waistline. Remove all gathering stitches.

SEWING THE BELL-BOTTOM LEGGINGS

8. As in making the sleeve extension, cut two pieces of tie-dye fabric according to Figure A. Measure the circumference of the child's leg, then add 1". That is Measurement A. Double that total to determine cutting Measurement B. Measure the length from the child's knee to the floor. Then add 2" to that total to arrive at cutting Measurement C. Cut the fabric from the bottom corners to the top measurement marks.

9. Finish the top and bottom edges. With right sides together, sew the angled side seams together and finish-stitch the edge. Turn the top edge under 2" and sew to create a casing, leaving an opening for the elastic. Measure the elastic around the child's leg to a tight but comfortable length and add 1". Thread the elastic through the casing and sew the ends together. Sew a narrow hem (see page 10) on the bottom edge.

SEWING THE HEADBAND SCARF

10. Cut the tie-dye fabric 44" wide by 5" to make a scarf that hangs long down the back. Fold and press the fabric strip lengthwise with right sides together. Sew a ¼" seam along the three open edges. Leave a section open to turn right side out. Clip the corners and turn right side out. Topstitch all the edges and close the opening. ■

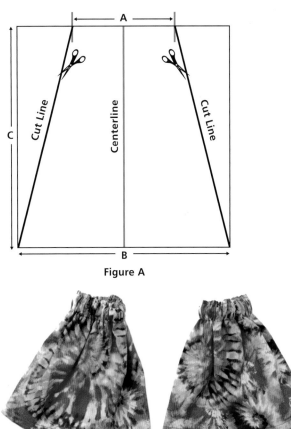

Figure A

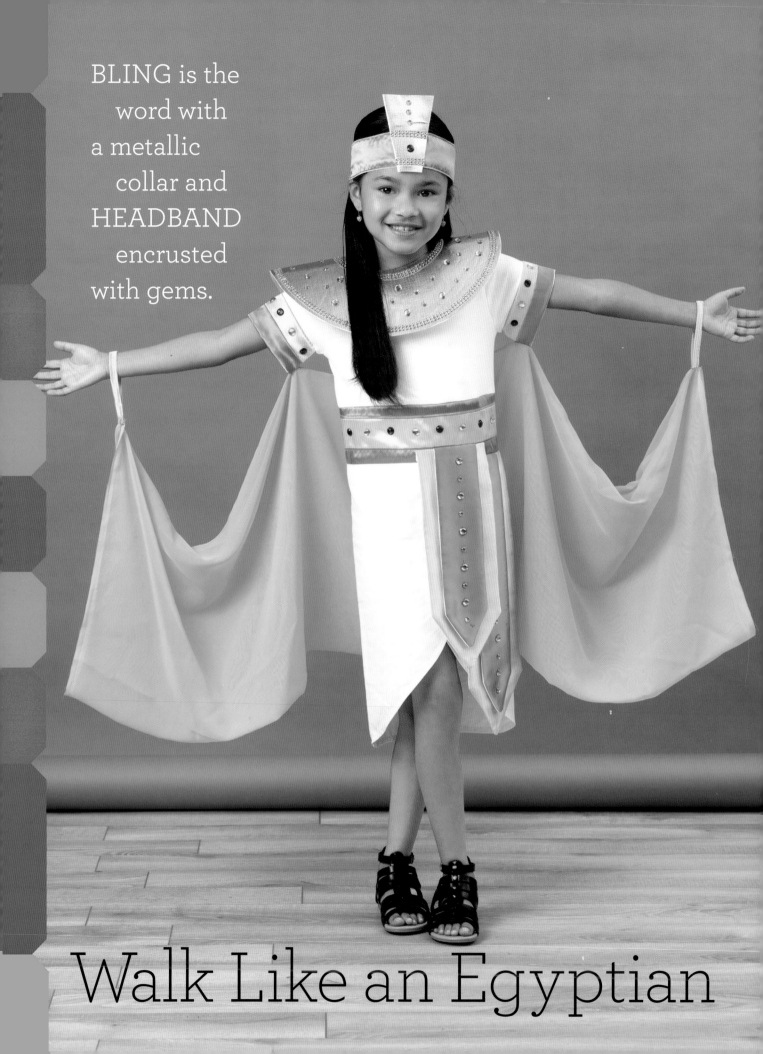

BLING is the word with a metallic collar and HEADBAND encrusted with gems.

Walk Like an Egyptian

Walk Like an Egyptian

Cleopatra would be proud to wear this authentic-looking design. Satin, rhinestones, and organza transform a humble white T-shirt into a garment fit for a queen.

Instructions are for sizes Small (Medium, Large, Extra-Large). Select the size to sew based on the closest matching chest measurement in the chart on page 6. All seam allowances are ½" unless otherwise noted.

WHAT YOU'LL NEED
- Basic tool kit (see page 7)
- Craft knife
- String and marking pen
- Narrow roller foot
- T-shirt: white, short sleeve
- White cotton (see yardage chart at right)
- Multicolored round glue-on rhinestones
- Gem glue
- 2 yards ⅜" rhinestone border trim tape
- Hook-and-loop strip, ½" wide by 1" long
- Hook-and-loop dot, ½"
- ½ yard 1" white braided elastic

For the belt, cuffs, and sash:
- ¾ yard 60"-wide gold satin
- ¾ yard 60"-wide turquoise satin

For the shawl:
- 1 yard 60"-wide turquoise organza
- ¼ yard ¾" yellow grosgrain ribbon

For the headband and collar:
- 2 white 2mm foam sheets, 9" x 12"
- ¾ yard 58"-wide metallic Oly-Fun fabric
- Egyptian medallion template (page 131)

44"-wide fabric	S (2/3)	M (4/5)	L (6/6x)	XL (7/8)
White cotton	1¼ yards	1¼ yards	1½ yards	1½ yards

PREPARING THE T-SHIRT

1. Lay the T-shirt out flat, measure and mark 2 (2½, 3, 3½)" down from each underarm seam, and follow the cutting instructions on page 6. Mark the center front and center back.

2. Cut any excess hem fabric from the sleeves. To determine the cutting width of the turquoise and gold satin and white cotton fabrics, measure the circumference of the sleeve opening and add 1". Cut the gold satin and the turquoise satin fabric length at 2". Cut the white cotton fabric length at 3". With right sides together, sew one long edge of the turquoise fabric to one long edge of the gold fabric. Press the seam flat. With right sides together, sew the other long turquoise fabric edge to the white cotton edge. With the right sides together, sew the short sides to make a circle. Turn right side out. With wrong sides together, fold the piece widthwise along the white fabric seam. Press and finish-stitch the edge. Fold the cuff into quarters and mark the sleeve openings. Matching the marks, sew the cuff to the T-shirt using a narrow zigzag stitch. Repeat to make the second cuff.

SEWING THE BELT

3. To determine the fabric cutting width of all belt pieces, measure the circumference of the T-shirt at the chest and add 2". Cut the gold satin length at 3". Cut two strips of the turquoise satin length at 2". Cut the white cotton length at 5". With right sides together, sew one long edge of each piece of turquoise satin to one long edge of the gold satin. Press and topstitch these seams. With wrong sides together, sew the satin fabric strip to the white cotton piece. Finish-stitch the edges. Sew the short ends right sides together, to create a circle. Fold the belt into quarters and mark the sides, front, and back center. Matching the marks, sew the belt to the T-shirt using a narrow zigzag stitch.

SEWING THE SKIRT

4. To determine the white skirt fabric cutting width, measure the circumference of the T-shirt at the chest and add 6". Use the chart below for the cutting length of the skirt.

	S (2/3)	M (4/5)	L (6/6x)	XL (7/8)
Skirt length	15"	16"	17"	19"

5. Fold the fabric in half widthwise and mark and cut a curved hemline as in Figure A. Finish-stitch along all the edges. Create a narrow hem (see page 10) on the curved edge. Lay the skirt fabric flat and overlap the front curved edges by 4". See Figure B for reference. Baste together the overlapping front edges.

6. To create the skirt sashes, cut two fabric pieces of the gold satin 6" x 17". Cut twp pieces of the turquoise satin 4" x 16". Then, cut two pieces of the white cotton fabric 6" x 17" and two pieces 4" x 16". As in Figure C, mark a centerline and measure up the side markings to form a point on each piece of white fabric. Matching the satin and the cotton pieces right sides together, sew along the angle marks, then sew a ½" seam along the two long sides. Trim ¼" from the angled seam and turn right side out. Press flat and center the turquoise sash inside the gold sash. Cut and shorten the length of one set of sashes by 3". Baste the pieces together and finish-stitch across the top edges. Position and baste the long sash off center of the skirt opening as in the photo.

ATTACHING THE SKIRT TO THE T-SHIRT

7. With right sides together, sew the skirt to the T-shirt belt, matching side front and back marks. Make sure to catch the top of the sash within the waistband seam. Position the second sash at the center and along the bottom of the belt strip. With right sides together, sew the sash in place.

8. Use gem glue to decorate the sleeves, belt, and sashes with round rhinestones.

9. To make the shawl, trim and square off the edges of the 1 yard of organza fabric. Narrow roller hem the short edges. Fold the fabric in half lengthwise with right sides together. Sew and finish the long edges. Turn the shawl right side out. Handstitch a loop of grosgrain ribbon to the seamed edge at each end. Lay the dress flat with the dress back side up. Loosely drape the fabric across and hand-tack the shawl edge to the bottom edge of the sleeves.

TIP
Lay a ruler along the edge you want to embellish to easily space a straight line of rhinestones.

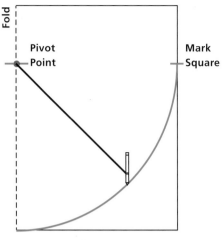

Figure A

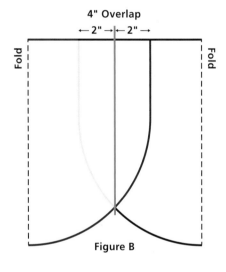

Figure B

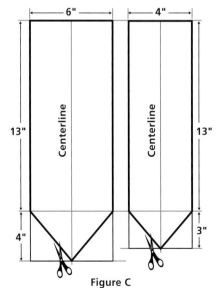

Figure C

Walk Like an Egyptian

MAKING THE GOLD COLLAR AND HEADBAND

10. Refer to Figure D to make the gold collar. To determine the center circle, measure across the front of the child's neck and add 1". Measure the child from shoulder to shoulder and add 3" to determine the outer circle. Lay the foam sheets side by side and tape together to achieve the width you need. Mark a center point with a pin attached to a string tied to a marking pen, then draw the neck and shoulder circles. Cut out the circles and a center split with a sharp craft knife. Lay the metallic Oly-Fun fabric flat over the entire foam circle, covering the marks and tape. Glue the fabric smoohtly to the foam shape. Let dry and trim the metallic fabric to the edges. Attach sticky back rhinestone tape around the edges and glue rhinestones in place. On the underside, stick a 1"-long hook-and-loop strip near the neck to make a collar closure at the split. To keep the collar from bouncing up in front, attach a hook-and-loop dot on the collar that aligns with a dot on the T-shirt.

11. To make the headband, cut a piece of the turquoise satin 3" x 12". Cut a white cotton fabric piece 3" x 12". Sew with right sides together, along the two long sides. Turn right side out and press flat. Turn the fabric ends of the tube inside ½". Copy and transfer the Egyptian medallion template onto the Oly-Fun fabric. Cut out the shape and fold along the dashed lines. Center the medallion on the headband and sew it to the top and bottom edges of the turquoise headband. Cover the seams with rhinestone tape and glue on round rhinestones. Cut a piece of the 1"-wide elastic to the circumference of the child's head minus the length of the turquoise headband piece. Sew to the inside of the ends of the headband. Topstitch the ends closed. ■

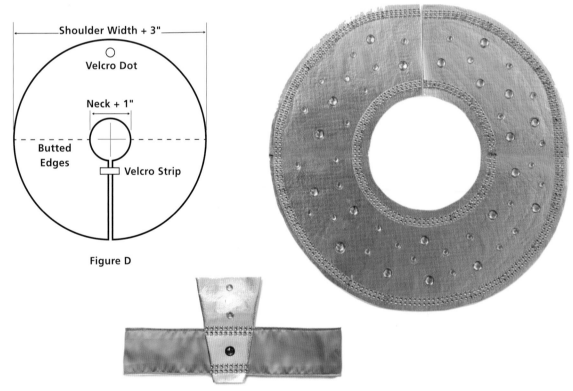

Figure D

SHIVER ME
timbers, that's one
cute PIRATE!

Ahoy, Mateys!

Ahoy, Mateys!

Pirates can be scary, but plenty of ruffles keep this little swashbuckler looking sweet. A faux belt with a shiny buckle and gold braid trim on the attached vest add sparkle.

Instructions are for sizes Small (Medium, Large, Extra-Large). Select the size to sew based on the closest matching chest measurement in the chart on page 6. All seam allowances are ½" unless otherwise noted

WHAT YOU'LL NEED
• Basic tool kit (see page 7)

• Craft knife

• T-shirt: white, long sleeve

For the skirt:
• Pink and black harlequin print cotton (see yardage chart at right)

• Black and white stripe cotton (see yardage chart at right)

• Pink and white double-pleated ruffle trim (see yardage chart at right)

For the vest and belt:
• Black microsuede (see yardage chart at right)

• 1½ yards gold trim

For the belt buckle:
• 9" x 12" white 3mm foam sheet

• ⅛ yard 30"-wide gold metallic Oly-Fun fabric

• Fabric glue

44"-wide fabric	S (2/3)	M (4/5)	L (6/6x)	XL (7/8)
Black and white stripes	¾ yard	1 yard	1 yard	1 yard
Pink and black harlequin print	½ yard	¾ yard	¾ yard	¾ yard

58"-wide fabric	S (2/3)	M (4/5)	L (6/6x)	XL (7/8)
Microsuede	½ yard	½ yard	½ yard	¾ yard

2"-wide trim	S (2/3)	M (4/5)	L (6/6x)	XL (7/8)
Pink ruffle	4 yards	4½ yards	4¾ yards	5 yards
White ruffle	½ yard	½ yard	½ yard	½ yard

PREPARING THE T-SHIRT
1. Lay the T-shirt out flat, measure and mark 3 (3½, 4, 4½)" down from each underarm seam, and follow the cutting instructions on page 6. Mark the center front and center back.

SEWING THE BODICE
2. To make the neck ruffle, cut two layers of harlequin print 5" square. Fold in half to find the center vertical line. On each side of the centerline, measure and mark 1½" on the top edge. Cut from each top edge mark to the bottom corners to create a trapezoid shape. With wrong sides together and using a ¼" seam, sew three edges of the shape, leaving the narrow top edge open. Clip the corners and turn the piece right side out. Fold the fabric top edge inside, press, and topstitch the edge closed. Cut three 5" strips each of the pink and the white ruffle trims. Alternating the color rows, sew the six rows of trim close together to the trapezoid piece. Trim off extra lengths and turn under the trim cut ends. Center and sew the neck ruffle to the T-shirt neckline.

3. Cut the pink ruffle to the circumference of the sleeve cuffs, plus 1" for overlapping the ends. Sew a ruffle to the edge of each sleeve.

MAKING THE VEST
4. To determine the cutting dimension for the microsuede vest, measure the T-shirt length from the shoulder to the cut waistline. Refer to the chart below for the fabric cutting width. Cut two layers.

	S (2/3)	M (4/5)	L (6/6x)	XL (7/8)
Vest width	24"	25"	27"	29"

5. Lay the T-shirt out and align the edge of a piece of paper down the front center of the T-shirt. Trim the paper width at the side seam. Feeling with your fingers through the paper, trace the approximate armhole curve, base of the neckline, and shoulder seam. Mark as in Figure A. Cut out the paper template. With two fabric layers, right sides together, trace the vest shape onto the microsuede fabric twice. Sew directly on the marking lines. Do not sew across the bottom edge. Trim ¼" from the sewn edges, clip the curved seam allowances, turn right side out, and press. Topstitch all the edges, turning under and closing the bottom edge.

6. Lay the vest pieces flat, reflecting both sides. Sew the gold trim ¼" from the curved edge of the vest. Handstitch the vest pieces to the shoulder and side seams.

SEWING THE SKIRT

7. Measure the circumference of the T-shirt at the chest and add 2" to determine the desired cutting width of the waistband. Cut the microsuede length at 5". Sew the short edges right sides together to create the back seam. To double the thickness, with wrong sides together, fold the band in half lengthwise. Baste-stitch and finish the edge. Fold to divide the waistband into quarters and mark the sides and front. Using a narrow zigzag stitch and matching the marks, sew the folded edge of the waistband to the T-shirt.

8. To determine the black and white striped fabric cutting width, measure the circumference of the T-shirt at the chest and multiply by 2½. If the width measurement is wider than the fabric width, divide that number in half. Then cut two fabric pieces and sew them together. This creates two side seams and prevents an awkward seam placement. Use the chart below to cut the underskirt length.

	S (2/3)	M (4/5)	L (6/6x)	XL (7/8)
Underskirt length	13"	14"	15"	17"

9. Measure the circumference of the T-shirt at the chest and multiply by 2½ to determine the harlequin print fabric cutting width. Use the chart below to cut the top-skirt length.

	S (2/3)	M (4/5)	L (6/6x)	XL (7/8)
Top-skirt length	6½"	7"	7½"	8½"

10. With both the underskirt and the top-skirt, finish-stitch along the top and bottom edges. With right sides facing, fold and sew the sides to create the back seam of each skirt. Narrow-hem (see page 10) the bottom edge of the skirts and sew the pink ruffled trim to the edge. Stack the two skirts, matching at the waistline edge. Along the waistline edge sew two rows of basting stitches for gathering; sew one row ¼" from the edge and the second row ¼" below that. Fold to divide the skirt into quarters and mark the sides and front.

ATTACHING THE SKIRT TO THE T-SHIRT

11. With right sides together, sew the skirt to the waistband. Use a ½" seam and match the sides, front, and back marks.

MAKING THE BELT BUCKLE

12. Using a sharp craft knife, cut a piece of foam sheet 2½" x 2". Glue the foam rectangle to the gold metallic fun fabric and trim it to the foam edges. Along the edges, place a ¾" mark in from all corners. Draw intersecting lines from edge to edge to create a 1" x ¾" rectangle in the center. Cut out the center opening. Use fabric glue to attach the buckle to the waistband. ■

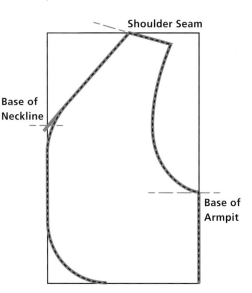

Figure A

TIP
You don't need to draw perfectly smooth curved lines when creating the template. Once sewn as a seam line, imperfections in the line will smooth out in the fabric.

Cat's Meow

This ADORABLE costume is just PURRFECT!

Cat's Meow

A pleated skirt and bow tie add a sophisticated touch to a cute and cuddly tiger cub. Substitute the orange stripes for a black T-shirt and leggings to turn a tiger into a black cat. It will look grrreat!

Instructions are for sizes Small (Medium, Large, Extra-Large). Select the size to sew based on the closest matching chest measurement in the chart on page 6. All seam allowances are ½" unless otherwise noted.

WHAT YOU'LL NEED
- Basic tool kit (see page 7)

- Craft knife

- Hot-glue gun and glue sticks

- T-shirt: orange, striped long sleeve

- Leggings: orange striped

For the skirt:
- Orange quilt cotton (see yardage chart at right)

For the belly bib:
- ¼ yard 44"-wide white cotton

For the tail:
- 8 ounces poly-fill batting

- ½ yard ⅜"-wide orange satin ribbon

For the headband:
- Orange satin ⅝" headband

- 1 each of 9" x 12" orange and pink 2mm foam sheets

- Tiger ears template (page 131)

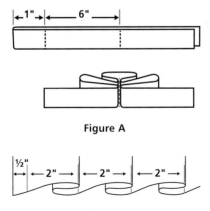

Figure A

Figure B

44"-wide fabric	S (2/3)	M (4/5)	L (6/6x)	XL (7/8)
Orange cotton	1 yard	1 yard	1 yard	1¼ yards

PREPARING THE T-SHIRT
1. Lay the T-shirt out flat, measure and mark 5½ (6, 6½, 7)" down from each underarm seam, and follow the cutting instructions on page 6. Mark the center front and center back.

SEWING THE BODICE
2. To make the belly bib, cut two layers of white fabric 5" x 6". Make a 3" circle paper template to mark and cut four rounded corners. With wrong sides together, using a ¼" seam, sew the edges of the shape, leaving the straight top edge open. Clip the corners and turn the piece right side out. Fold the fabric top edge inside, press, and topstitch the edge closed. Center and sew the belly bib to the T-shirt neckline.

3. To make a bow, cut a piece of orange cotton fabric 3" x 18". Fold the fabric pieces right sides together lengthwise. Sew around three sides of the fabric strip, leaving a small opening in the seam. Clip the corners and turn the fabric strip right side out. Press and topstitch the edges.

4. Referring to Figure A, fold the fabric strip in half. Sew across the strip 1" from the folded edge, then again at 6" from that sewn line. Open the loops and stack the seams to create a bow. Handstitch the bow to the center neckline.

SEWING THE SKIRT
5. To determine the orange fabric cutting width, measure the circumference of the T-shirt at the chest, multiply by 2, then add 2". If the width measurement is wider than the fabric width, divide that number in half. Then cut two fabric pieces and sew them together. This prevents an awkward seam placement. Use the chart below to cut the skirt length.

	S (2/3)	M (4/5)	L (6/6x)	XL (7/8)
Skirt length	10"	11"	12"	14"

6. Finish-stitch along the top edge. Fold to divide the skirt into quarters and mark the sides and front. Narrow-hem (see page 10) the bottom edge of the skirt.

7. Lay the skirt fabric flat; starting at the fabric left edge, place a mark ½" from the top and bottom edges. Continue to place marks every 2" along the top and bottom edges. Referring to Figure B, fold from left to right and match every other mark to create 2" pleats. Pleats may not evenly work out across the width. You can adjust the widths of the last two pleats at the right side. This will be less visible at the back seam edge. Press the pleats flat. Baste-stitch the pleats flat near the waistband and at the hem. (This makes it easier to sew the skirt to the T-shirt.) With right sides facing, fold and sew the sides together to create the back seam of the skirt.

ATTACHING THE SKIRT TO THE T-SHIRT
8. With right sides together, matching the sides, front, and back marks and using a narrow zigzag stitch, sew the skirt to the T-shirt. Remove all visible basting stitches.

MAKING THE TAIL
9. Cut the orange cotton fabric 6" x 24" to make a tail. (The length may be adjusted here if you don't want the tail to drag.) Fold the fabric pieces with right sides together lengthwise. On the short edge of one side, measure and mark 1" from the fold.

10. Cut an angle from that 1" mark to the other short 3" edge. This create a long triangle shape. Sew a ½" seam down the cut edge, and turn right side out. Loosely fill the tail with batting. Make sure to not overstuff the tail, especially near the top. This will be for comfort as well as allowing the tail to fall straight down under the skirt. Turn in the fabric edges and sew the end closed. Handstitch several strips of ribbon and a bow to the tip. Handstitch the tail to the rear center seam of the leggings.

MAKING THE HEADBAND
11. Copy and tape the tiger ears template piece (1) to the orange foam sheet and piece (2) to the pink foam sheet. Cut out the ear pieces with a sharp craft knife. Hot-glue the pink shape to the center of the orange ear shape as the template dotted lines indicate. Cut a split down the bottom center. To form a cup shape, bend the earpiece toward the centerline and overlap the bottom cut edges until it become a straight edge. Glue the overlapped edges together. Repeat for the second ear. Then position and glue the ears to the headband. ■

Light up
HER FACE
with a
Jack-o'-Lantern
SMILE.

Lil' Pumpkin

Lil' Pumpkin

Pick this little dress to stand out from the rest of the patch. This classic Halloween costume gets a fresh look with a bubble skirt and fleece beret.

Instructions are for sizes Small (Medium, Large, Extra-Large). Select the size to sew based on the closest matching chest measurement in the chart on page 6. All seam allowances are ½" unless otherwise noted.

WHAT YOU'LL NEED
- Basic tool kit (see page 7)
- Marking pen and string
- Craft knife
- T-shirt: orange, long sleeve

For the bodice:
- Pumpkin face template (page 132)
- 2 black 5" x 7" iron-on twill patches

For the skirt:
- Orange quilt cotton (see yardage chart at right)
- 1 yard 54"-wide white nylon netting

For the hat:
- Orange polar fleece fabric (see yardage chart at right)
- Six 12" green 6mm chenille stems

44"-wide fabric	S (2/3)	M (4/5)	L (6/6x)	XL (7/8)
Orange cotton	1 yard	1½ yards	1¾ yards	1¾ yards

58"-wide fabric	S (2/3)	M (4/5)	L (6/6x)	XL (7/8)
Polar fleece	¾ yard	¾ yard	1 yard	1 yard

PREPARING THE T-SHIRT
1. Lay the T-shirt out flat, measure and mark 4 (4½, 5, 5½)" down from each underarm seam, and follow the cutting instructions on page 6. Mark the center front and center back.

2. Copy and cut out the pumpkin face template and lightly tape it over the black twill iron-on patches. With a sharp craft knife, carefully cut out the shapes. Place the cutout shapes onto the center front of the T-shirt and press in place. Follow the product instructions for pressing time.

SEWING THE SKIRT
3. The skirt is constructed from two layers: a top skirt and an underskirt. For the top skirt, measure the circumference of the T-shirt at the chest and multiply by 3 to determine the orange fabric cutting width. If the width measurement is wider than the fabric width, divide that number in half, then cut two fabric pieces and sew them together. This creates two side seams and prevents an awkward seam placement. Use the chart below to cut the skirt length.

	S (2/3)	M (4/5)	L (6/6x)	XL (7/8)
Skirt length	12"	13"	14"	15"

4. Finish-stitch along the top and bottom edges. With right sides facing, fold and sew the short edges to create the back seam of the top skirt. On the top and bottom edges, sew two rows of basting stitches for gathering; sew one row ¼" from the edge and the second row ¼" below that. Fold the top skirt to divide into quarters and mark the sides and front.

5. To determine the cutting width for the underskirt, measure the circumference of the T-shirt at the chest and add 2". Use the same chart above to cut the skirt length.

6. Finish-stitch along the top and bottom edges. With right sides facing, sew the short edges together to create the center back seam. Fold to divide the underskirt into quarters and mark the sides and front.

7. Pull the basting threads to gather one edge of the top skirt. With right sides together, matching marks, sew the top skirt edge to the underskirt edge. Turn the skirts right side out. Cut the nylon netting into random-size strips and crumple, adjusting the desired fullness to place between the two skirt layers. With the wrong sides together, matching marks, sew the top skirt top edge to the underskirt top edge. Remove all the gathering stitches.

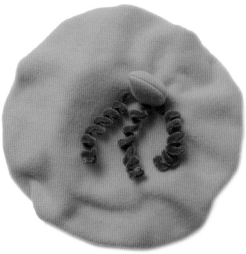

ATTACHING THE SKIRT TO THE T-SHIRT

8. With right sides together, matching the sides, front, and back marks and using a ½" seam, sew the skirt waistband to the T-shirt with a narrow zigzag stitch.

SEWING THE HAT

9. Measure the circumference of the child's head and add 3". Cut the orange fleece fabric length at 5" to make the headband. Sew the short edges together to create a circle. Fold in half, widthwise, to create a double-thick headband. Check for fit, adjusting at the seam. Baste-stitch the edges together. Fold the headband into quarter segments and mark the sides, front, and back.

10. Cut a square piece of orange fleece fabric according to the chart below.

	S (2/3)	M (4/5)	L (6/6x)	XL (7/8)
Fleece square	18" x 18"	20" x 20"	23" x 23"	23" x 23"

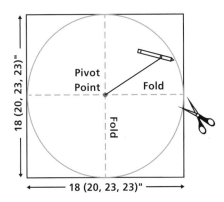

Figure A

11. Find the center point of the square by folding the fabric twice. Refer to Figure A and place a pin at the pivot point. With a marking pen attached to a string that measures from the center pivot point to the edge of the fabric, draw a circle. Cut out the circle and sew two rows of basting stitches around the circumference for gathering; sew one row ¼" from the edge and the second row ¼" below that. Fold the fabric into quarter segments and mark the sides, front, and back.

12. Pull the basting threads to gather the edges of the hat. With right sides together, matching marks, sew the hat to the headband.

13. Twist two chenille stems together to form one thick stem. At one end, form a circle about the thickness of your finger. Make two more double-thick stems. Twist to attach the ends of each stem to the circle. Twist each stem around a pencil to create a spiral. Pull open the spiral as desired. Sew the chenille stem circle to the hat.

14. To make the pumpkin stem, cut the polar fleece fabric 4" x 3". Fold the fabric to be 2" wide. Draw a rounded top corner as in Figure B. Trim and sew a ¼" seam from the edge. Turn the stem right side out. Turn under the bottom edge and sew the stem to the hat, covering the inner circle of stems. ■

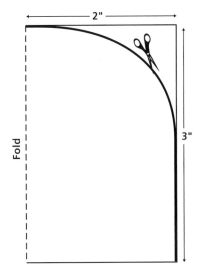

Figure B

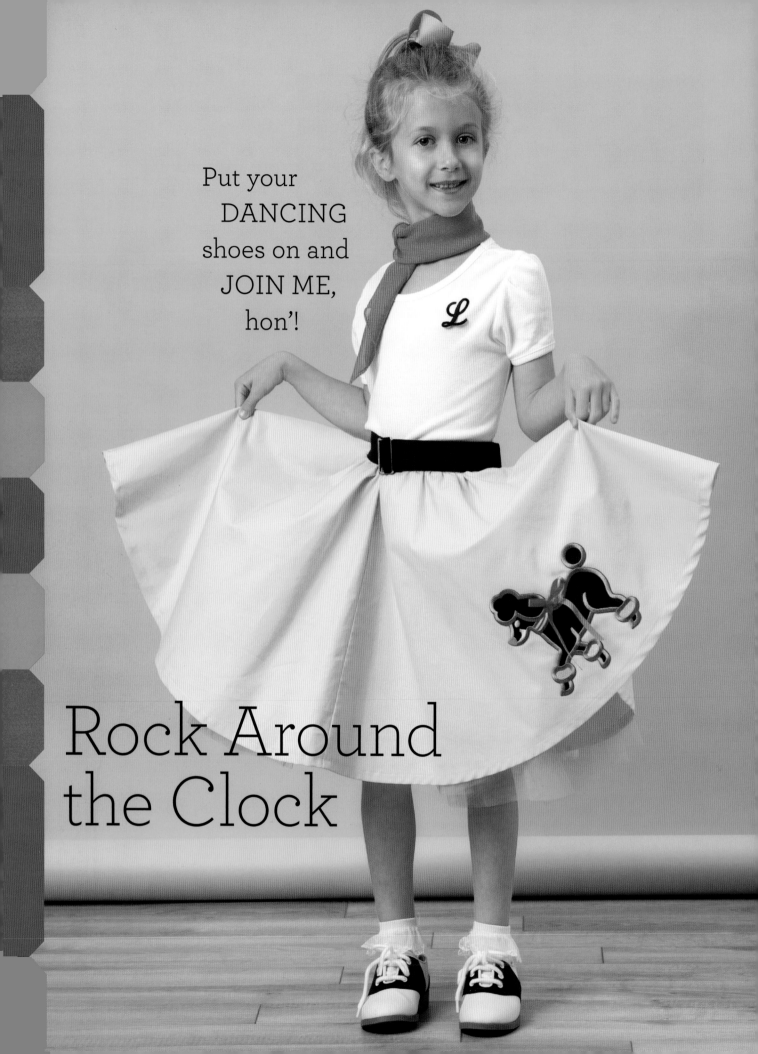

Put your
DANCING
shoes on and
JOIN ME,
hon'!

Rock Around the Clock

Rock Around the Clock

A full circle skirt buoyed by layers of netting will let her dance till broad daylight, or at least until bedtime. Change the monogram to match your little rock 'n roller's name.

Instructions are for sizes Small (Medium, Large, Extra-Large). Select the size to sew based on the closest matching chest measurement in the chart on page 6. All seam allowances are ½" unless otherwise noted.

WHAT YOU'LL NEED

- Basic tool kit (see page 7)
- String and marking pen
- T-shirt: white, puffy short sleeve
- Black monogram iron-on letter

For the skirt:
- Pink cotton fabric (see yardage chart at right)
- Pink nylon netting (see yardage chart at right)
- Iron-on poodle appliqué
- ½ yard ⅜" pink satin ribbon

For the belt:
- ¼ yard 44"-wide black canvas fabric
- Cinch belt buckle with 1½" opening

44"-wide fabric	S (2/3)	M (4/5)	L (6/6x)	XL (7/8)
Pink cotton	1½ yards	1½ yards	2¾ yards	3 yards

54"-wide fabric	S (2/3)	M (4/5)	L (6/6x)	XL (7/8)
Pink netting	2½ yards	2¾ yards	5¾ yards	6 yards

PREPARING THE T-SHIRT

1. Lay the T-shirt out flat, measure and mark 4 (4½, 5, 5½)" down from each underarm seam, and follow the cutting instructions on page 6. Mark the center front and center back.

2. On the upper left side of the chest, follow the product instructions and iron on the monogram letter.

SEWING THE SKIRT

3. To determine the pink fabric cutting width to make the waistband, measure the circumference of the T-shirt at the chest and add 2". Cut the fabric length at 4". With right sides facing, sew the short edges of the waistband together to create the center back seam. Fold the band in half lengthwise and sew with wrong sides together to create a double-thick waistband. Fold to divide the waistband into quarters and mark the sides and front.

4. To make the nylon netting underskirt, measure the circumference of the T-shirt at the chest and multiply by 4 to determine the fabric cutting length. For the Small and Medium sizes, fold the netting lengthwise, twice. This creates four layers. For the Large and Extra-Large sizes, stack two lengths of tulle and fold in half lengthwise to create four layers. Along the folded long edge, sew two rows of basting stitches for gathering; sew one row ¼" from the edge and a second row ¼" below that. Refer to the chart below for the netting fabric cutting width. Fold the underskirt to divide into quarters and mark the sides, front, and back.

	S (2/3)	M (4/5)	L (6/6x)	XL (7/8)
Netting width	12"	13"	14"	16"

5. Pull the gathering threads to match the side and center markings to the waistband. Starting at the back, sew the netting piece flat to the waistband.

6. Refer to the chart below for the pink skirt cutting measurements. Cut one large square piece of the pink fabric. If the width measurement is wider than the fabric, divide only the width number in half. Then cut two fabric pieces and sew them together. This creates a seam on the sides and prevents an awkward seam placement.

	S (2/3)	M (4/5)	L (6/6x)	XL (7/8)
Skirt cutting dimensions	40" x 40"	42" x 42"	46" x 46"	50" x 50"

7. Referring to Figure A, fold the fabric into quarters to find the center pivot point. With a string attached to a marking pen, draw a round corner. Cut through all layers to create a full circle hemline.

8. Refer to the chart below for the measurement to mark on the edge. From the same center fold pivot point, with a string attached to a marking pen, draw a round corner to cut for the skirt waistline.

	S (2/3)	M (4/5)	L (6/6x)	XL (7/8)
Skirt waist depth	4"	4"	5"	5"

9. On the inner circle edge, sew two rows of basting stitches for gathering; sew one row ¼" from the edge and the second row ¼" below that. Fold to divide the skirt into quarters and mark the sides, front, and back. Create a narrow hem (see page 10) on the outer circle edge.

ATTACHING THE SKIRT TO THE T-SHIRT
10. Pull the basting threads to gather the skirt waistline. With the right sides together, sew the waistband and skirt together, matching the side, front, and back marks. Remove all the gathering stitches.

11. With right sides together, and using a narrow zigzag stitch and matching the side, front, and back marks, sew the waistband to the T-shirt.

APPLYING THE POODLE APPLIQUÉ
12. Position the poodle appliqué off center and toward the hem of the skirt. Follow the product instructions and iron on the poodle. Handstitch a pink ribbon bow to the appliqué.

MAKING THE BELT
13. To make the detached adjustable belt, cut the black canvas fabric width to the circumference of the T-shirt waist and add 6". For a 1½" buckle opening, cut the fabric length at 3½". Fold the fabric lengthwise with right sides together. Sew a ¼" seam along the three cut edges, leaving an open space in the seam. Clip the corners and turn the belt right side out. Press and topstitch all the edges, closing the opening. Loop one end of the belt around the center bar of the buckle and sew a reinforced seam close to the buckle. Weave the other end through the buckle and cinch the belt to fit. ■

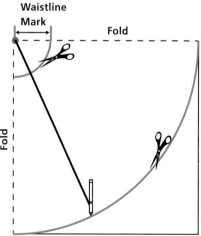

Figure A

Over the Rainbow

She'll skip down the YELLOW brick road in this pretty PINAFORE.

This little
WITCH
is more SWEET
than wicked.

Spellbound

Spellbound

The cutest little witch to ever fly on a broomstick, she's positively bewitching in dramatic full sleeves and a black cat–print pinafore. Orange rickrack and oversized buttons brighten up this classic costume.

Instructions are for sizes Small (Medium, Large, Extra-Large). Select the size to sew based on the closest matching chest measurement in the chart on page 6. All seam allowances are ½" unless otherwise noted.

WHAT YOU'LL NEED
• Basic tool kit (see page 7)

• T-shirt: black, long sleeve

For the sleeves and skirt:
• Black quilt cotton (see yardage chart at right)

• Orange dotted quilt cotton (see yardage chart at right)

For the apron:
• Halloween print cotton (see yardage chart at right)

• 1½ yards ½"-wide orange rickrack

• 2 round orange buttons

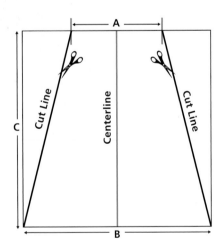

Figure A

44"-wide fabric	S (2/3)	M (4/5)	L (6/6x)	XL (7/8)
Black cotton	1½ yards	2 yards	2 yards	2¼ yards
Orange dotted fabric	¾ yard	¾ yard	¾ yard	1 yard
Halloween print	1¼ yards	1¼ yards	1½ yards	1½ yards

PREPARING THE T-SHIRT
1. Lay the T-shirt out flat, measure and mark 3 (3½, 4, 4½)" down from each underarm seam, and follow the cutting instructions on page 6. Mark at the center front and center back.

SEWING THE BODICE
2. To create the waistband belt, cut the length of the orange dot fabric at 2½". Measure the circumference of the T-shirt at the chest and add 2" to determine the fabric cutting width. Sew the short edges with right sides together to create a circle. Finish-stitch around both edges. Fold the waistband into quarters and mark the sides, front, and back center. With right sides together, matching the marks, sew the waistband to the T-shirt using a narrow zigzag stitch.

SEWING THE SLEEVE EXTENSIONS
3. Cut off the existing hem of the T-shirt sleeves. Cut two pieces of black fabric according to Figure A to create the sleeve extensions. To determine the cutting dimensions, measure the circumference of the T-shirt sleeve opening, then add 1". Consider that total cutting Measurement A. Double that total to determine cutting Measurement B. Measure the length between the child's armpit to the wrist. Subtract the length of the existing sleeve from the armpit to the T-shirt edge. Then add 1" to that total to arrive at cutting Measurement C. Cut the fabric from the corner to the top measurement marks.

4. Finish the top and bottom edges. With right sides together, sew the angled side seams together and finish the edge. Sew a narrow hem (see page 10) on the bottom edge. Fold to divide the sleeve extension and T-shirt sleeve into quarters to mark the bottom (side seam), top, front, and back. With right sides together, using a narrow zigzag stitch and matching marks, sew the sleeve extension to the sleeve.

SEWING THE APRON
5. Paying attention to the direction of the Halloween print pattern, cut two pieces of fabric according to the chart below for the apron.

	S (2/3)	M (4/5)	L (6/6x)	XL (7/8)
Apron skirt dimensions	14" x 14"	15" x 15"	16" x 16"	17" x 17"

6. With one layer of fabric, sew a double row of rickrack trim 2" from the bottom edge. With fabric pieces right sides together, sew around three sides, leaving the top open. Clip the corners and turn right side out. Press and topstitch along the three edges. Finish the top edge of the apron and sew two rows of basting stitches for gathering; sew one row ¼" from the edge and the second row ¼" below that.

Spellbound

7. Cut two pieces of Halloween print fabric according to the chart below to create the bib. With one layer of fabric, sew rickrack trim 1½" from the top and bottom edges. With the fabric pieces right sides together, sew around three sides of the bib, leaving the bottom open. Clip the corners and turn right side out. Press and topstitch along the three edges. Finish the bottom edge of the bib.

	S (2/3)	M (4/5)	L (6/6x)	XL (7/8)
Apron bib dimensions	7" x 7"	7½" x 7½"	8" x 8"	8½" x 8½"

8. Fold and mark the center of the apron and the bib. Sew the apron and bib with right sides together, pulling the gathering threads and matching the marks. Sew the apron and bib seam centered horizontal and vertically within the waistband.

9. To make the shoulder and apron straps, cut two strips of Halloween fabric according to the chart below. Pay attention to fabric pattern direction. Fold lengthwise and press each fabric strip with right sides together. Sew a ¼" seam along three open edges. Leave a small section in the seam open to turn right side out. Clip the corners and turn right side out. Press and topstitch along all edges. Sew a long strap to each edge of the bib next to the apron seam. Handstitch a short strap to each T-shirt shoulder seam. Lay the T-shirt flat and position and sew the straps behind the bib at each top corner. Center the buttons in line with the straps and handstitch in place.

	S (2/3)	M (4/5)	L (6/6x)	XL (7/8)
Shoulder straps	3" x 5½"	3" x 6"	3" x 6½"	3" x 7"
Apron straps	22" x 3"	23" x 3"	25" x 3"	27" x 3"

SEWING THE SKIRT

10. To make the skirt ruffle, cut orange dot fabric to the width measurements in the chart below by a 6" length. Cut and sew together extra strips to obtain the total length. Fold in half lengthwise and press to create a double-thickness ruffle. Finish the edge and sew two rows of basting stitches for gathering; sew one row ¼" from the edge and the second row ¼" below that. Fold to divide into quarters and mark the sides and front center seam.

	S (2/3)	M (4/5)	L (6/6x)	XL (7/8)
Ruffle width	110"	116"	126"	136"

11. Measure the circumference of the T-shirt at the chest and multiply by 2½ to determine the black skirt fabric cutting width. If the width measurement is wider than the fabric width, divide that number in half. Then cut two fabric pieces and sew them together. This creates two side seams and prevents an awkward seam placement. Use the chart below to cut the skirt length.

	S (2/3)	M (4/5)	L (6/6x)	XL (7/8)
Skirt length	16"	18"	19"	21"

12. Finish-stitch along the top and bottom edges. With right sides facing, fold and sew the sides to make the back seam of the skirt. On the waistline edge, sew two rows of basting stitches for gathering; sew one row ¼" from the edge and the second row ¼" below that. Fold to divide the skirt into quarters and mark the sides, front, and back. Matching marks, sew the ruffle to the hem edge. Press flat and edgestitch along the seam to keep it lying flat.

ATTACHING THE SKIRT TO THE T-SHIRT

13. Pull the threads to gather the skirt waistline. With right sides together and matching marks, sew the skirt to the T-shirt waistband. Remove all gathering stitches. ◼

TIP
Long, straight blunt-end tweezers help with turning straps right side out. Pulling the fabric through by grabbing it from the inside is easier than trying to push it through with a pencil.

With ruffled trims and SEQUINS, she will SPARKLE like the heavens.

Sweet Angelica

Sweet Angelica

Your little one might not always be a perfect angel, but she can look like one! Detachable wings and a ruffled halo add an ethereal look. Leave off the wings and halo for a lovely first communion or flower girl dress.

Instructions are for sizes Small (Medium, Large, Extra-Large). Select the size to sew based on the closest matching chest measurement in the chart on page 6. All seam allowances are ½" unless otherwise noted.

WHAT YOU'LL NEED
- Basic tool kit (see page 7)
- Narrow roller foot
- Wire cutters
- Craft knife
- Hot-glue gun and glue sticks
- T-shirt: white, puffy short sleeve

For the skirt:
- White satin charmeuse (see yardage chart at right)
- ½ yard 1½"-wide white satin ribbon

For the bodice and wings:
- 4 yards ¾" white special pleated satin trim

For the skirt and wings:
- White sequin open-weave fabric (see yardage chart at right)

For the wings:
- 4 yards 16-gauge craft wire
- Glitter glue
- 2 yards ⅛"-wide white cording

For the halo:
- White headband
- 1 yard 2"-wide white double-pleated ruffle trim

54"-wide fabric	S (2/3)	M (4/5)	L (6/6x)	XL (7/8)
White satin charmeuse	1½ yards	1½ yards	1¾ yards	1¾ yards

58"-wide fabric	S (2/3)	M (4/5)	L (6/6x)	XL (7/8)
White sequin open-weave	2 yards	2 yards	2¼ yards	2½ yards

PREPARING THE T-SHIRT
1. Lay the T-shirt out flat, measure and mark 4 (4½, 5, 5½)" down from each underarm seam, and follow the cutting instructions on page 6. Mark the center front and center back.

SEWING THE BODICE
2. To determine the cutting length of the bodice trim, measure the distance from the shoulder seam to the center front of the T-shirt waistline and add 1". Cut two pieces of the special pleated trim. Pin one piece of trim 1" out from the center waistline mark and sew down the center of the trim to the shoulder seam. Fold under the rough-cut trim end. Repeat for the opposite shoulder.

3. To make the bow tie, cut the 1½" satin ribbon to 8". Sew the cut ends together to form a loop. Use a zigzag stitch to prevent fraying. Lay the loop flat with the seam centered at the back. Cut a 2" length of ribbon and fold in half widthwise to make a ¾"-wide center piece of the bow. Zigzag stitch the short ends closed. Wrap the ribbon center piece around the center of the loop piece. Pinch and tighten the center piece until the loop edges bend in slightly. Handstitch the center piece and the loop piece together to secure the shape. Handstitch the bow to the front of the T-shirt neckline.

4. For the wing's anchor loops, cut two pieces of cording 2" long. Fold each into a loop and handstitch one to each T-shirt shoulder seam with the loop lying down the back. Wrap the thread around the cording ends several times to keep a neat cut end and prevent fraying.

SEWING THE SKIRT
5. To determine the waistband satin fabric cutting width, measure the circumference of the T-shirt at the chest and add 2". Cut the waistband length at 5". With right sides facing, sew the short edges together to create the center back seam. Fold in half lengthwise, with wrong sides together, baste, and finish the edges to form a double-thickness waistband. Fold the waistband to divide into quarters and mark the sides and front.

6. Measure the circumference of the T-shirt at the chest and multiply by 3 to determine the satin fabric cutting width. Use the chart below to cut the skirt length.

	S (2/3)	M (4/5)	L (6/6x)	XL (7/8)
Skirt length	16"	18"	20"	24"

Sweet Angelica

7. Finish-stitch along the top edges. With right sides facing, fold and sew the sides to make the back seam of the skirt. Fold to divide the skirt into quarters and mark the sides, front, and back. Narrow-hem (see page 10) the bottom edge of the skirt.

MAKING THE SHEER OVERSKIRT

8. To determine the cutting width of the sequin open-weave fabric, measure the circumference of the T-shirt at the chest and multiply by 3. Use the skirt length chart above to cut the sheer overskirt length.

9. Fold the fabric in half widthwise. Mark on the fabric folded edge half the length of the overskirt. Refer to Figure A, and cut a freehand curve from the folded edge down to the bottom. Lay the fabric out flat and use a narrow roller foot to hem the curve edge.

10. Finish-stitch the top and side edges. With right sides facing, sew the short edges together to create the center back seam.

ATTACHING THE SKIRTS TO THE WAISTBAND

11. Matching the back seams, stack and baste together the overskirt to the skirt at the waistline edges. On the waistline edge, sew two rows of basting stitches for gathering; sew one row ¼" from the edge and the second row ¼" below that.

12. Pull the basting threads to gather the skirt waistline. With right sides together, sew the skirt to the waistband, matching the side, front, and back marks. Remove all the gathering stitches.

ATTACHING THE SKIRT TO THE T-SHIRT

13. With right sides together, sew the waistband to the T-shirt, using a narrow zigzag stitch and matching the sides, front, and back marks.

MAKING THE WINGS

14. Refer to Figure B and bend the 16-gauge wire to create the wing starting shape that encompasses a 20" x 20" area. Make sure the connecting point of the ends of the wire twist and overlap on one of the wing edges, not the 2" center horizontal section. Once the starting shape is symmetrical, bend and smooth the straight vertical wires to shape into softer shape wings (Figure C). Like snowflakes, no two angel wings are exactly the same.

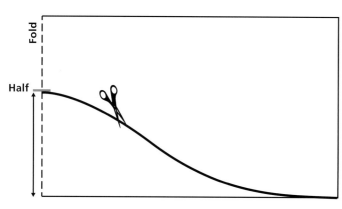

Figure A

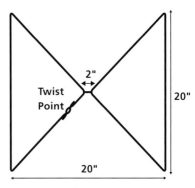

Figure B

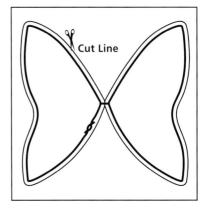

Figure C

TIP
A cutting mat with 1" grid markings is a helpful guide to construct symmetrical wings.

15. Cut the sequin open-weave fabric to a 22" square. With right side up, center the wire structure over the sequin open-weave fabric. About every 2", spaced out around the wing shapes, using small dots, hot-glue the wire to the fabric. Trim the fabric ½" from the outside edge of the wire. Fold the fabric edges over the wire, pulling the fabric taut, and place small glue dots to secure the fabric to the top of the wire. Starting at the 2" center horizontal wire, hot-glue the white special pleated trim to cover the wire edges. Cut the trim once you've completed gluing all the way around. Do not cover the center 2" horizontal wire. Do the same for the edges of the other wing. Once the glue is dry, turn the structure over and lay flat. With glitter glue, run a narrow bead of glue tracing the wire structure for both wings.

16. Find the center of the remaining white cording and cut it in two pieces. Hold the wing structure midway between the top of each wing tip to the horizontal center wire. Adjust your hand positions until you feel a natural balancing point where the wings hang straight up and down without tilting forward or back. Mark and hot-glue one end of each cording to those positions. Lace the cording strands through each T-shirt shoulder loop. Tie in a bow at the shoulder.

MAKING THE HALO
17. Bend and twist together the 16-gauge wire to create a 10" circle. At the twisted connecting point of the wire, leave a straight 10" wire that sticks out from the circle. Starting at the stem and using the widest zigzag stitch, slowly sew the double-pleated ruffle trim to the wire. The zigzag needle will alternately catch one stitch on each side of the wire as you sew down the center double seam of the ruffle. There will be ease enough in the seam to bunch and gather the trim as you sew. Gather and sew the entire ½ yard of ruffle trim.

18. Twist the stem around the center of the headband and straighten the halo. ■

Busy Bee

Everyone will
be BUZZING
about this sweet
little BUG.

Busy Bee

Detachable wings, fluttery shoulder ruffles, and
layers of frothy tulle let your little girl flit and fly from
flower to flower. It's as cute as can bee!

Instructions are for sizes Small (Medium, Large, Extra-Large). Select the size to sew based on the closest matching chest measurement in the chart on page 6. All seam allowances are ½" unless otherwise noted.

WHAT YOU'LL NEED
• Basic tool kit (see page 7)

• Zipper foot

• Hot-glue gun and glue sticks

• Wire cutters

• T-shirt: black, sleeveless

• 1½ yards 1½" yellow grosgrain ribbon

For the skirt:
• Yellow cotton fabric (see yardage chart at right)

• Yellow tulle (see yardage chart at right)

• Black sheer glitter wire ribbon (see yardage chart at right)

For the wings:
• ½ yard 60" black organza

• 5 feet 16-gauge craft wire

• 2 yards ½" black double-fold bias tape

• 2 yards ⅛" black cording

44"-wide fabric	S (2/3)	M (4/5)	L (6/6x)	XL (7/8)
Yellow cotton	1 yard	1 yard	1 yard	1¼ yards

54"-wide fabric	S (2/3)	M (4/5)	L (6/6x)	XL (7/8)
Yellow tulle	3¾ yards	4 yards	6¼ yards	6¾ yards

⅝"-wide trim	S (2/3)	M (4/5)	L (6/6x)	XL (7/8)
Sheer glitter wire	5½ yards	5¾ yards	8½ yards	9 yards

PREPARING THE T-SHIRT
1. Lay the T-shirt out flat, measure and mark 4½ (5, 5½, 6)" down from each underarm seam, and follow the cutting instructions on page 6. Mark the center front and center back.

SEWING THE BODICE
2. Measure at the side seams across the chest of the T-shirt to determine the length to cut two strips of grosgrain ribbon and add 1". Position at the underarm seams and sew on both long edges of one ribbon. Turn under the cut ends and sew down the T-shirt side seam. Sew the second ribbon strip ½" below that strip.

3. On the back of the T-shirt, measure from the top of the shoulder to the center mark of the T-shirt cut waistline. Cut two strips of grosgrain ribbon to that measurement and add 1". Position and pin both ribbons to be next to each other at the waistline and angle out toward the shoulders. Turn under the ribbon end and sew to the shoulder seam. For smaller shirt sizes, fold the ribbon edge under to taper the ribbon width if needed. Sew the ribbons in place on both long edges.

4. For the wing's anchor loops, cut three pieces of cording 2" long. Fold each into a loop and handstitch one to each shoulder seam and one in the center of the T-shirt back, at the underarm height. Wrap the thread around the cording ends several times to keep a neat cut end and prevent fraying.

5. Make two shoulder ruffles: Measure from the center of the front armhole over the shoulder to the center back of the armhole. Cut two pieces of bias tape to that length. Cut two pieces of the yellow netting twice the length of the bias tape by 8" wide. Fold the netting in half lengthwise. Sew two lines of basting stitches ¼" apart, along the folded edge. Pull the threads and gather the netting. Evenly space the ruffles along the inside of the double-folded bias tape. Sandwich the netting ruffle inside and sew the bias tape together. Handstitch the ruffles along the shoulder and armhole seam.

SEWING THE SKIRT
6. To determine the cutting width for the waistband, measure the circumference of the T-shirt at the chest and add 2". Cut the yellow fabric waistband length at 5". With right sides facing, sew the short edges together to create the center back seam. Fold in half lengthwise, with wrong sides together, baste-stitch, and finish the edge. Fold the waistband to divide into quarters and mark the sides and front.

Busy Bee

7. Measure the circumference of the T-shirt at the chest and multiply by 2½ to determine the yellow fabric cutting width. If the width measurement is wider than the fabric width, divide that number in half. Then cut two fabric pieces and sew them together. This creates two side seams and prevents an awkward seam placement. Use the chart below to cut the underskirt length.

	S (2/3)	M (4/5)	L (6/6x)	XL (7/8)
Underskirt length	12 "	13 "	14 "	16 "

8. Finish-stitch along the top and bottom edges. With right sides facing, fold and sew the short sides together to create the back seam of the underskirt. On the waistline edge, sew two rows of basting stitches for gathering; sew one row ¼ " from the edge and the second row ¼ " below that. Fold to divide the skirt into quarters and mark the sides and front. Narrow-hem (see page 10) the bottom edge of the skirt.

9. To make three tulle pieces, measure the circumference of the T-shirt at the chest and multiply by 3 to determine the fabric cutting length.

For the Small and Medium sizes: Cut two pieces of tulle fabric. Fold one piece of tulle lengthwise twice to create four fabric layers. Sew one row of basting stitches along the folded edge and cut according to the chart for the bottom piece width. Repeat the folding for the second piece of tulle. Sew one row of basting stitches along both long sides and cut to the middle piece width. Create the top piece by trimming the long side of the remaining piece according to the chart.

For the Large and Extra Large sizes: Cut three pieces of tulle fabric. Stack two pieces of tulle and fold lengthwise to create four fabric layers. Sew one row of basting stitches along both long sides and cut according to the chart below for the bottom piece width. Create the top pieces by trimming the long side of the remaining piece according to the chart. Fold one piece of tulle lengthwise twice to create four fabric layers. Sew one row of basting stitches along the fold edge and cut to the middle piece width.

	S (2/3)	M (4/5)	L (6/6x)	XL (7/8)
Top width	4 "	4 "	4 "	5 "
Middle width	8 "	9 "	10 "	11 "
Bottom width	12 "	13 "	14 "	16 "

10. Using a narrow zigzag stitch, sew the sheer glitter wire ribbon to the top layer of each tulle piece. Stack the three tulle pieces at the baste-stitched edge and sew two rows of basting stitches for gathering; sew one row a ¼ " from the edge and the second row ¼ " below that. Fold to divide the tulle skirt into quarters and mark the sides and front.

11. Pull the gathering threads to match the sides and center markings. Starting at the back seam, sew the tulle skirt to the underskirt, as close as possible to the skirt gathering stitches.

12. Pull the gathering threads on the underskirt to match the sides and center markings and sew the underskirt to the waistband. Make sure this seam includes the top edge of the tulle skirt. Remove all gathering stitches.

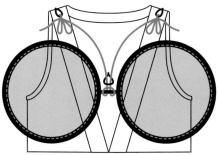

Figure A

TIP
When hand-tacking pieces in place, use a contrasting color thread for easy removal later.

ATTACHING THE SKIRT TO THE T-SHIRT

13. With right sides together, and using a ½" seam, sew the folded edge of the waistband to the T-shirt. Use a narrow zigzag stitch and match the sides, front, and back marks.

MAKING THE WINGS

14. With the craft wire, shape and twist a 10" circle with a 2" straight stem out to the side. Cut two layers of black organza 12" square. Baste-stitch along the edges of the two layers to keep them from slipping apart. Center the wire circle in the middle of the fabric square. About every 2", spaced out around the circle, using small dots, hot-glue the wire to the organza. Trim the organza ½" from the outside of the wire. Fold the edges over the wire, pulling the fabric taut, and place small glue dots to secure the fabric to the top of the wire. Starting at the stem, hand-tack the bias tape in place as you cover the circle edges. Sandwich the wire between the folds of the bias tape. Once you've wrapped the circle edges, leave an extra 3" of bias tape at the end. Using a zipper foot, sew the edge of the bias tape. Repeat to make the second wing.

15. Securely twist the two circle wire stems together and wrap the excess bias tape to cover the joint. Fold under and handstitch all bias-tape edges. Remove the tacking stitches.

16. Refer to Figure A for the wing attachment. Find the center of the remaining black cording and tie to the center stems of the wings. Lace the strings through the center loop on the back of the T-shirt. Pull one strand up through each shoulder loop. Tie in a bow at the shoulder. ∎

Tiaras and
PEARLS
aren't just for
PRINCESSES!

Glamour
Girl

Glamour Girl

She may be mistaken for a movie star, whether she's having breakfast at Tiffany's or a Happy Meal with her mom. Satin bows and a tulle peplum really glam up a simple sleeveless T-shirt.

Instructions are for sizes Small (Medium, Large, Extra-Large). Select the size to sew based on the closest matching chest measurement in the chart on page 6. All seam allowances are ½" unless otherwise noted.

WHAT YOU'LL NEED
• Basic tool kit (see page 7)

• T-shirt: black, sleeveless

• Black double-faced satin ribbon (see yardage chart at right)

For the skirt:
• Black quilt cotton (see yardage chart at right)

• Black tulle (see yardage chart at right)

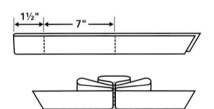

Figure A

44"-wide fabric	S (2/3)	M (4/5)	L (6/6x)	XL (7/8)
Black cotton	½ yard	½ yard	¾ yard	¾ yard

54"-wide fabric	S (2/3)	M (4/5)	L (6/6x)	XL (7/8)
Black tulle	3¾ yards	4 yards	4¼ yards	4½ yards

⅞"-wide ribbon	S (2/3)	M (4/5)	L (6/6x)	XL (7/8)
Black double-faced satin	3 yards	3 yards	3¼ yards	3¼ yards

PREPARING THE T-SHIRT
1. Lay the T-shirt out flat, measure and mark 4 (4½, 5, 5½)" down from each underarm seam, and follow the cutting instructions on page 6. Mark the center front and center back.

2. Cut at an angle two strands of satin ribbon 30" long. Referring to Figure A, fold the ribbon in half. Sew across 1½" from the folded edge, then again at 7" from that sewn line. Open the loops and stack the seams to create a bow. Make two bows and handstitch them to the shoulder seams.

SEWING THE SKIRT
3. To determine the skirt cotton fabric cutting width, measure the circumference of the T-shirt at the chest and add 2". Use the chart below for the cutting length.

	S (2/3)	M (4/5)	L (6/6x)	XL (7/8)
Skirt length	14"	15"	16"	18"

4. Finish-stitch along the top and bottom edges. With right sides facing, fold and sew the sides to make the back seam of the skirt. On the waistline edge, sew two rows of basting stitches for gathering; sew one row ¼" from the edge and the second row ¼" below that. Fold to divide the skirt into quarters and mark the sides, front, and back. Create a narrow hem (see page 10) on the bottom edge.

5. To make two tulle pieces, measure the circumference of the T-shirt at the chest and multiply by 3 to determine the fabric cutting length. Fold one piece of tulle lengthwise twice to create four fabric layers. Sew two rows of basting stitches for gathering; sew one row ¼" from the folded edge and the second row ¼" below that. Cut the width in the chart below, measuring from the basting seam. Repeat for the second tulle piece. Fold each piece to divide into quarters and mark the center and side seams.

	S (2/3)	M (4/5)	L (6/6x)	XL (7/8)
Tulle width	10"	11"	12"	13"

6. Pull the basting threads to gather. Pin and match the sides and center markings. Starting at the back, sew one tulle piece flat to the underskirt below the double-baste stitching on the underskirt edge. To alternate the open short edges between the pieces, start at the side seam and sew the second piece of tulle beneath the first tulle piece. Fluff and separate the fabric layers for fullness.

ATTACHING THE SKIRT TO THE T-SHIRT

7. Pull the threads to gather the skirt waistline. With right sides together, sew the skirt to the T-shirt, making sure to catch the top layer of tulle within the seam. Use a small zigzag stitch, matching the sides, front, and back marks. Remove all gathering stitches.

8. Tie a black ribbon sash around the waist. Cut the ribbon to the desired length at an angle to prevent the ends from fraying. Hand-tack it to the waistband at the side seams. ■

TIP
To add more fluff to the tulle layers, sew the second layer underneath at the same location, but upside down. This actually folds the tulle over the seam that the layer was sewn on with.

NIGHTTIME
is not
REST time
for this
fearless crime
fighter.

Night Flyer!

Night Flyer!

Made with a turtleneck and stretchy jersey knit, this comfy costume will keep your little one warm, whether she's fighting crime or trick-or-treating. The scalloped wings are attached to keep her hands free to fly.

Instructions are for sizes Small (Medium, Large, Extra-Large). Select the size to sew based on the closest matching chest measurement in the chart on page 6. All seam allowances are ½" unless otherwise noted.

WHAT YOU'LL NEED
- Basic tool kit (see page 7)
- Craft knife
- String and marking pen
- T-shirt: black, long-sleeve turtleneck

For the skirt and wings:
- Black jersey-knit fabric (see yardage chart at right)
- 5" circle template

For the bat appliqué:
- Bat symbol template (page 132)
- Pink glitter iron-on transfer sheet

For the mask:
- Bat mask template (page 133)
- 9" x 12" black 2mm foam sheet
- ¼" paper punch
- ½ yard ½" black elastic

60"-wide fabric	S (2/3)	M (4/5)	L (6/6x)	XL (7/8)
Black jersey knit	1½ yards	1¾ yards	2 yards	2 yards

PREPARING THE T-SHIRT
1. Lay the T-shirt out flat, measure and mark 4 (4½, 5, 5½)" down from each underarm seam, and follow the cutting instructions on page 6. Mark the center front and center back.

2. Copy the bat symbol template and lightly tape it over the iron-on transfer sheet. With a sharp craft knife, carefully cut out the appliqué. Place it on the center front of the T-shirt and follow the product instructions for pressing time.

SEWING THE SKIRT
3. Measure the circumference of the T-shirt at the chest and multiply by 1½ to determine the desired cutting width of the jersey fabric skirt. Refer to the chart below for the cutting length. (In a later step, you will be cutting into this overall skirt length to create a shorter front hem length.)

	S (2/3)	M (4/5)	L (6/6x)	XL (7/8)
Skirt length	19"	20"	22"	24"

4. With right sides facing, sew the short edges together to create the center back seam. As in Figure A, mark a centerline to indicate the sides of the skirt. Refer to the chart below to measure and mark the front skirt length.

	S (2/3)	M (4/5)	L (6/6x)	XL (7/8)
Front length	12"	13"	15"	17"

5. Referring to Figure A, measure and mark a line 2" from the back seam. Noting where marking lines intersect, draw a curved line from high to low for a smooth hem-edge transition. Narrow-hem (see page 10) the cut edge of the skirt.

6. On the waistline edge, sew two rows of basting stitches for gathering: one row ¼" from the edge and the second row ¼" below that. Fold to divide the skirt into quarters and mark the sides, front, and back.

ATTACHING THE SKIRT TO THE T-SHIRT
7. Pull the basting threads to gather the skirt waistline. With the right sides of the T-shirt and skirt together, sew a ½" seam, using a narrow zigzag stitch and matching the sides, front, and back marks. Remove all the gathering stitches.

SEWING THE BAT WINGS (MAKE 2)
8. Lay the dress flat with the T-shirt arms straight out to the sides. Measure the depth of the dress from the armpit to the short (front) hem and the length of the inside sleeve seam. With right sides together, cut two rectangles of black jersey knit to these measurements. Sew the long edges of the rectangle together.

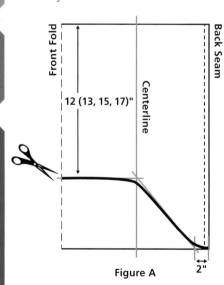

Front Fold

Back Seam

12 (13, 15, 17)"

Centerline

Figure A

2"

9. Referring to Figure B, measure and mark a square in the lower portion of the rectangle to find a pivot point. With a string attached to a marking pen, draw a curve. Make a 5" paper circle template, then align and mark circles centered along the curved edge. Pin and sew directly on the marked scalloped lines. Trim a ¼" edge close to the sewn line. Snip and clip the curved seam allowance. Turn the wing right side out and press flat. Turn the short edge under and topstitch all the edges of the wing. Repeat Steps 8 and 9 to make a second wing.

10. Lay one wing flat, matching the straight edges of the wing with the side of the dress and the sleeve seam. Starting at the armpit, with the widest setting, zigzag stitch the wing along the sleeve edge. The zigzag needle will alternately catch one stitch on the wing, then the next stitch on the sleeve, continuing to sew the two pieces together. Return to the armpit and zigzag stitch along the dress edge. Repeat for the second wing.

MAKING THE MASK

11. Copy and tape the bat mask template to the black foam sheet. Cut out the mask with a sharp craft knife and punch the slots in the sides with a paper punch. Cut a 14" piece of elastic. Loop the elastic through the side slits and sew the elastic ends to secure to the mask. ■

Pivot Point

Main Square

5" Circles

Figure B

TIP
Cut the circle template out of stiff paper or thin cardboard to make tracing easier.

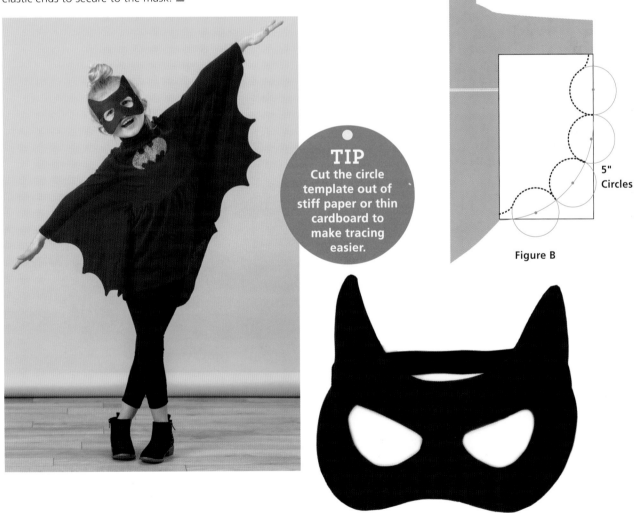

Show your TEAM pride by customizing the COLORS.

Good Cheer

Good Cheer

Every little girl will want to jump, shout, and cheer in this fan-favorite outfit. Authentic pleats add flair when she cartwheels and twirls.

Instructions are for sizes Small (Medium, Large, Extra-Large). Select the size to sew based on the closest matching chest measurement in the chart on page 6. All seam allowances are ½" unless otherwise noted.

WHAT YOU'LL NEED
• Basic tool kit (see page 7)

• T-shirt, white, V-neck, short sleeve

For the skirt and sash:
• Orange quilt cotton (see yardage chart at right)

• ¼ yard 44"-wide black quilt cotton

For the sleeve and skirt trim:
• ¾ yard ⅜"-wide orange grosgrain ribbon

• ⅞"-wide black grosgrain ribbon (see yardage chart at right)

44"-wide fabric	S (2/3)	M (4/5)	L (6/6x)	XL (7/8)
Orange quilt cotton	¾ yard	¾ yard	1 yard	1 yard

⅞"-wide trim	S (2/3)	M (4/5)	L (6/6x)	XL (7/8)
Black ribbon	2 yards	2¼ yards	2¼ yards	2½ yards

PREPARING THE T-SHIRT
1. Lay the T-shirt out flat, measure and mark 4 (4½, 5, 5½)" down from each underarm seam, and follow the cutting instructions on page 6. Mark the center front and center back.

SEWING THE BODICE
2. To determine the fabric cutting length for the front sash, measure from the neckline shoulder edge across the chest to the side seam, and add 1". The cutting width is determined by measuring the shoulder seam to the edge of the collar then adding 1". Cut two pieces of the orange fabric. With right sides together, sew a ½" seam on two edges to create a long tube. Turn the tube right side out and press flat.

3. Sew the black grosgrain ribbon ⅛" from each edge. Lay it flat and position the sash across the T-shirt. Fold the fabric inside the tube, starting at ½", and tuck more inside the tube to match the shoulder angle. Press flat and topstitch the edge. Handstitch the top edge to the shoulder seam. Baste-stitch the bottom to the T-shirt waistline.

4. Measure the circumference of the T-shirt sleeve opening, then add 1". Cut two lengths of the black and orange grosgrain ribbon to that measurement. Center the narrow orange ribbon on the wide black ribbon and sew both long edges. On both edges of the black ribbon, use a small zigzag stitch and sew it to the T-shirt sleeves. Overlap the ribbon ends at the seam. Try not to stretch the fabric too much as you sew.

SEWING THE SKIRT
5. Use the chart below to cut four orange fabric pieces for the skirt panels. With a ½" seam, sew the long edges of the four panels together, stopping to backstitch and secure 6" from one edge. To check for fit, measure the circumference of the T-shirt at the chest and add 1". Compare this measurement to the four panels sewn together. Make any needed adjustments evenly at the seams. Finish-stitch the waistline edge. Fold the skirt into quarters and mark the sides, front, and back center.

	S (2/3)	M (4/5)	L (6/6x)	XL (7/8)
Skirt panels (4)	7" x 12"	7¼" x 13"	7¾" x 14"	8¼" x 16"

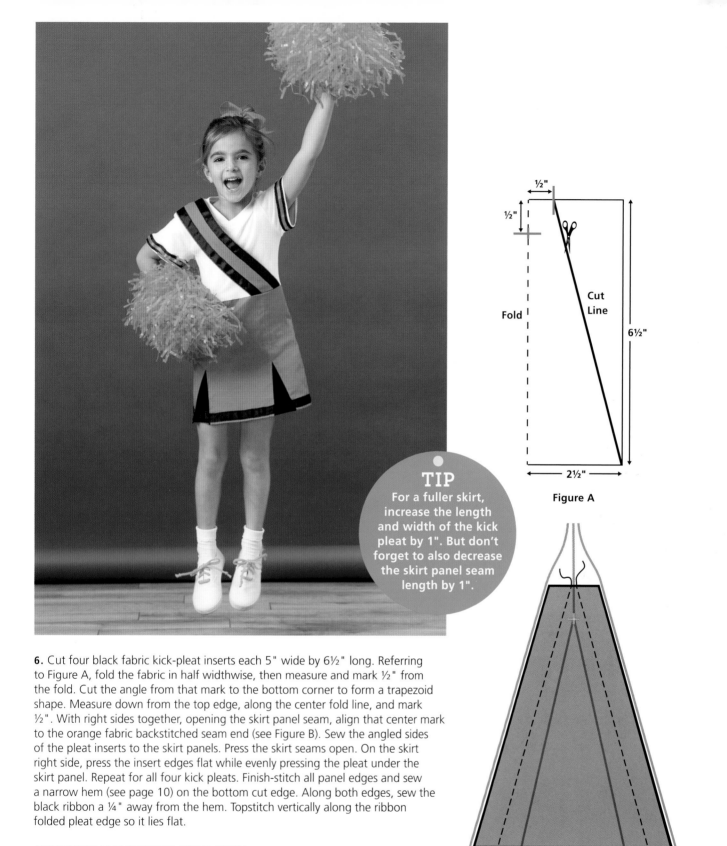

TIP
For a fuller skirt, increase the length and width of the kick pleat by 1". But don't forget to also decrease the skirt panel seam length by 1".

½"

½"

Fold

Cut
Line

6½"

2½"

Figure A

Figure B

6. Cut four black fabric kick-pleat inserts each 5" wide by 6½" long. Referring to Figure A, fold the fabric in half widthwise, then measure and mark ½" from the fold. Cut the angle from that mark to the bottom corner to form a trapezoid shape. Measure down from the top edge, along the center fold line, and mark ½". With right sides together, opening the skirt panel seam, align that center mark to the orange fabric backstitched seam end (see Figure B). Sew the angled sides of the pleat inserts to the skirt panels. Press the skirt seams open. On the skirt right side, press the insert edges flat while evenly pressing the pleat under the skirt panel. Repeat for all four kick pleats. Finish-stitch all panel edges and sew a narrow hem (see page 10) on the bottom cut edge. Along both edges, sew the black ribbon a ¼" away from the hem. Topstitch vertically along the ribbon folded pleat edge so it lies flat.

ATTACHING THE SKIRT TO THE T-SHIRT
7. With right sides together, sew the skirt to the T-shirt, using a small zigzag stitch and matching the sides, front, and back marks. ∎

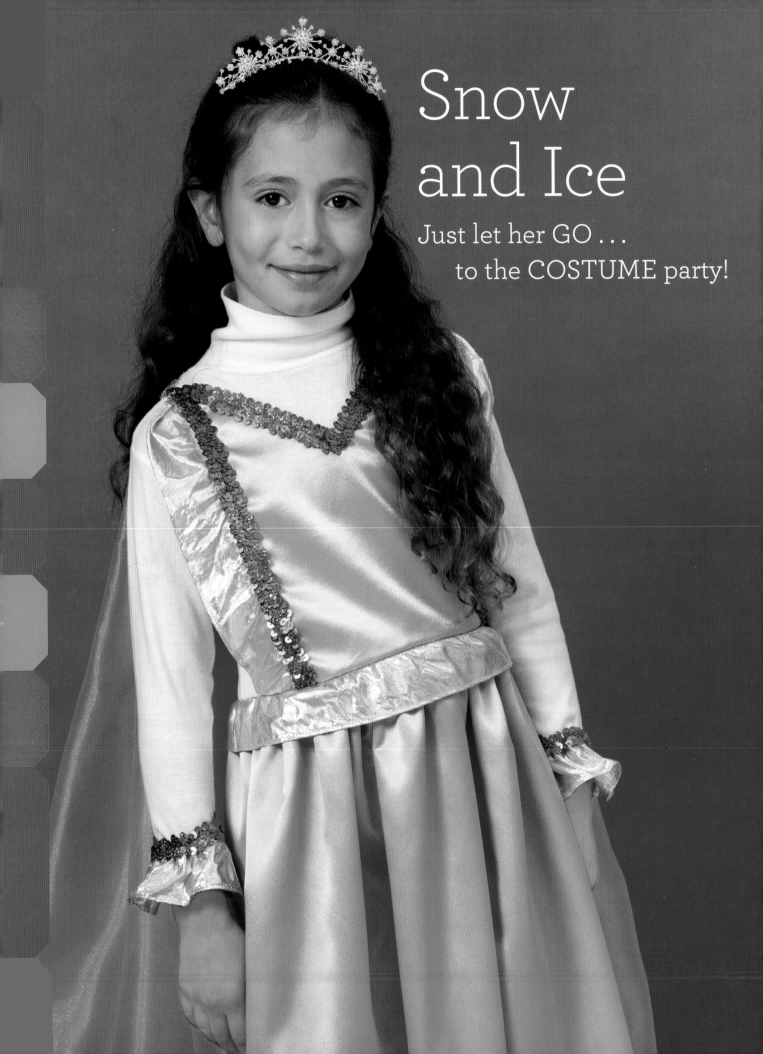

Snow and Ice

Just let her GO …
to the COSTUME party!

Snow and Ice

She doesn't have to freeze to be an elegant ice princess.
She'll shine in this sparkling costume of satin, organza, lamé,
and sequins anchored by a cozy turtleneck.

Instructions are for sizes Small (Medium, Large, Extra-Large). Select the size to sew based on the closest matching chest measurement in the chart on page 6. All seam allowances are ½" unless otherwise noted.

WHAT YOU'LL NEED
• Basic tool kit (see page 7)

• Narrow rolled hem foot

• T-shirt: white, long-sleeve turtleneck

For the bodice and skirt:
• Ice-blue satin (see yardage chart at right)

For the cape:
• Ice-blue organza (see yardage chart at right)

For the bodice trim and cuffs:
• 1¾"-wide silver ruffled lamé trim (see yardage chart at right)

• ⅞"-wide aqua sequin stretch trim (see yardage chart at right)

For the bodice:
• 14" x 14" square lightweight iron-on interfacing

TIP
To machine-sew the stretchy sequin trim, gently pull the sequins to the sides to reveal a center double seam. Sew between the seams, then push the sequins back into place.

	S (2/3)	M (4/5)	L (6/6x)	XL (7/8)
54"-wide satin fabric	1¼ yards	1½ yards	1¾ yards	2 yards
60"-wide organza	¾ yard	¾ yard	1 yard	1 yard
1¾"-wide ruffled trim	1¾ yards	1¾ yards	2¼ yards	2½ yards
⅞"-wide sequin trim	2½ yards	2½ yards	2¾ yards	3 yards

PREPARING THE T-SHIRT
1. Lay the T-shirt out flat, measure and mark 4 (4½, 5, 5½)" down from each underarm seam, and follow the cutting instructions on page 6. Mark the center front and center back.

SEWING THE BODICE
2. To determine the cutting width for the dress bodice, measure the distance between the center of the T-shirt shoulder seams and add 1". For the cutting length, measure from the top of the shoulder to the trimmed waistline and add 1".

3. On the wrong side of the satin fabric, follow the product instructions and iron on the interfacing. Finish-stitch the two side edges, turn under, and press flat. Sew the ruffle trim to each side. Sew the sequin trim on top of the ruffle trim.

4. To create a V neckline, fold the bodice panel in half to create the centerline. Measure from the T-shirt armpit to the T-shirt waist. Transfer that measurement to the center fold line and mark the bodice. Lay the bodice out flat. Staystitch a "V" line from the center point of that mark to the top corners of the bodice panel. Zigzag stitch along the outside of the staystitch edge. Sew the sequin trim to the inside edge of the "V" stitching, extending it past the top shoulder corners.

5. Cut the bodice fabric along the outside zigzag line to open up a V neckline. Hand-sew the extended sequin trim to the shoulders, tacking the ruffle edges under. Baste-stitch the bodice to the T-shirt waist. Using narrow zigzag stitches, sew the ruffle trim around the T-shirt waistline.

TRIMMING THE CUFFS
6. Cut 2" off each T-shirt cuff. Sew the ruffle trim to the sleeve edge. Overlap and finish the ruffle edges. To make a slightly tight cuff, pull and stretch the sequin trim as you sew it close to the ruffle edge.

SEWING THE SKIRT
7. Measure the circumference of the T-shirt at the chest and multiply by 3 to determine the satin skirt fabric cutting width. Use the chart below to cut the skirt length.

	S (2/3)	M (4/5)	L (6/6x)	XL (7/8)
Skirt length	22"	24"	26"	30"

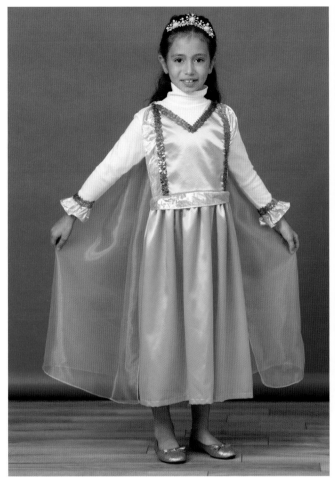

8. Finish-stitch along the top and bottom edges. With right sides facing, fold and sew the short edges together to make the back seam. On the waistline edge, sew two rows of basting stitches for gathering. Sew one row ¼" from the edge and the second row ¼" below that. Fold to divide the skirt into quarters and mark the sides, front, and back. Create a narrow-hem (page 10) on the bottom edge.

ATTACHING THE SKIRT TO THE T-SHIRT

9. Pull the basting threads to gather the skirt waistline. With right sides together, sew the skirt to the T-shirt, using a narrow zigzag stitch and matching the sides, front, and back marks. Remove all the gathering stitches.

SEWING THE CAPE

10. Cut the organza fabric using the chart below for the fabric width and measuring from the shoulders to the dress hemline and add 2" to determine the cutting length of the cape.

	S (2/3)	M (4/5)	L (6/6x)	XL (7/8)
Cape width	40"	50"	60"	60"

11. Narrow roll hem all four edges. At the top edge of the cape, starting from each side of the fabric and working toward the center, accordion-fold the organza into 2"-wide pleats. Lightly press at the top and pin to hold.

12. Measure the seam at the base of the turtleneck, from shoulder to shoulder. Cut the silver ruffled trim to that measurement. Lay the trim flat, then evenly space and sew the pleated organza cape to the wrong side of the trim. Turning under the trim rough edges, handstitch the cape to the seam across the back of the T-shirt neck. ■

TIP
For an easier start to your narrow rolled hem, fold and press a ¼" edge for a few inches, then the sewing foot will continue on its own.

117

It's a BIRD.
It's a plane.
IT'S A
preschooler!

Girl Power!

Girl Power!

Fueled by juice boxes and layers of tulle and netting, this tiny superhero won't be stopped. Gold accents add just the right amount of bling.

Instructions are for sizes Small (Medium, Large, Extra-Large). Select the size to sew based on the closest matching chest measurement in the chart on page 6. All seam allowances are ½" unless otherwise noted.

WHAT YOU'LL NEED
• Basic tool kit (see page 7)

• Craft knife

• T-shirt: blue, long sleeve

• 3 red iron-on embroidered stars

• Narrow-rolled hem foot

For the cape:
• Red silky charmeuse (see yardage chart at right)

• ½ yard ½"-wide seam tape

For the waistband and cuffs:
• ¼ yard 45"-wide gold metallic spandex

For the skirt:
• Red tulle (see yardage chart at right)

• Red nylon netting (see yardage chart at right)

For the star appliqué:
• Metallic gold iron-on transfer sheet

• Superhero star template (page 134)

60"-wide fabric	S (2/3)	M (4/5)	L (6/6x)	XL (7/8)
Red charmeuse	1 yard	1¼ yards	1¼ yards	1½ yards
Red tulle	3¾ yards	4 yards	4¼ yards	4½ yards
Red nylon netting	2 yards	2 yards	2¼ yards	2¼ yards

PREPARING THE T-SHIRT
1. Lay the T-shirt out flat, measure and mark 2½ (3, 3½, 4)" down from each underarm seam, and follow the cutting instructions on page 6. Mark at the center front and center back.

2. Copy the superhero star template and lightly tape it over the metallic gold iron-on transfer sheet. With a sharp craft knife, carefully cut out the shape. Place it on the center front of the T-shirt and follow the product instructions for pressing time.

3. Cut 2" off each sleeve cuff. Cut two pieces of metallic gold spandex 5" by the sleeve wrist measurement plus 1" for the seam. Sew the short edges with right sides together to create a circle. With wrong sides together, fold in half lengthwise to create a double-thickness cuff. With a narrow zigzag stitch, sew a cuff to each sleeve. Center a red embroidered star to the outside of each cuff, and follow the product instructions for pressing time.

SEWING THE SKIRT
4. Measure the circumference of the T-shirt at the chest and add 2" to determine the gold metallic spandex fabric cutting width. Cut the length at 6". Sew the short edges, right sides together, to create a circle. Fold in half lengthwise, wrong sides together, to create a double-thickness waistband. Baste-stitch and finish the edge. Fold the waistband into quarters and mark the sides, front, and back center. With right sides together and matching marks, use a narrow zigzag stitch to sew the waistband to the T-shirt. Topstitch the seam edge.

5. Measure the circumference of the T-shirt at the chest and multiply by 1½ to determine the red charmeuse underskirt fabric cutting width. Use the chart below to cut the length.

	S (2/3)	M (4/5)	L (6/6x)	XL (7/8)
Underskirt length	10"	11"	12"	13"

6. Finish-stitch along the top and bottom edges. With right sides together, fold and sew the short sides to make the back seam of the skirt. On the waistline edge, sew two rows of basting stitches for gathering; sew one row ¼" from the edge and the second row ¼" below that. Fold to divide the skirt into quarters and mark the sides, front, and back. Create a narrow hem (see page 10) on the bottom edge.

Girl Power!

7. To make two tulle pieces and one netting piece, measure the circumference of the T-shirt at the chest and multiply by 3 to determine the fabric cutting length. Fold one piece of tulle lengthwise twice to create four fabric layers. Sew two rows of basting stitches for gathering: sew one row ¼" from the folded edge and the second row ¼" below that. Cut the width in the chart below, measuring from the basting seam. Repeat for the second piece of tulle and the netting. Fold each piece to divide into quarters and mark the center and side seams.

	S (2/3)	M (4/5)	L (6/6x)	XL (7/8)
Tulle and netting width	10"	11"	12"	13"

8. Pull the basting threads to gather. Pin and match the sides and center markings. Starting at the back, sew one tulle piece flat to the underskirt below the double-baste stitching on the underskirt edge. To alternate the open short edges between the pieces, starting at the side seam, sew the second piece of tulle beneath the first tulle piece. Start at the other side seam to sew the netting piece beneath both tulle pieces. Fluff and separate the fabric layers for fullness.

ATTACHING THE SKIRT TO THE T-SHIRT

9. Pull threads to gather the underskirt waistline. With right sides together, sew the skirt to the waistband, making sure to catch the top layer of tulle within the seam; use a narrow zigzag stitch, matching sides, front, and back marks. Remove all gathering stitches.

MAKING THE CAPE

10. Measure from the shoulder to the hem of the dress and add 2" for the length of the cape. Cut the red charmeuse fabric width according to the chart below. As in Figure A, mark along the edge of the fabric 10" from each side. Cut from the mark to the corner to create a trapezoid shape. Use a narrow-rolled hem foot to finish all four side edges. Along the top shorter edge, fold the edge over and sew a 1½" hem. Within that hem, close to the seam, sew two rows of basting stitches ¼" apart for gathering.

	S (2/3)	M (4/5)	L (6/6x)	XL (7/8)
Cape width	50"	50"	60"	60"

11. Measure the back neck length plus 3" to cut the seam binding tape. Pull the threads to tightly gather the cape fabric edge. Sew the cape to the seam binding tape. Turning under the rough edges, handstitch the cape to the back of the T-shirt neck and 1" around the front collar.

MAKING THE HEADBAND

12. Measure the circumference of the child's head to determine the cutting width of the metallic spandex fabric. Cut the length at 5". With right sides together, fold the fabric in half and sew the long edges together to create a tube. Turn the tube right side out and turn in a ½" edge on one end. Tuck the other end inside the tube and handstitch the ends together. Attach the remaining red star in the center. ■

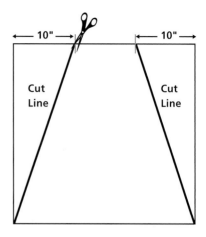

Figure A

TIP
If you don't want the cape permanently attached to the dress, sew a long narrow red charmeuse sash (see page 11) and sew the gathered cape fabric to it.

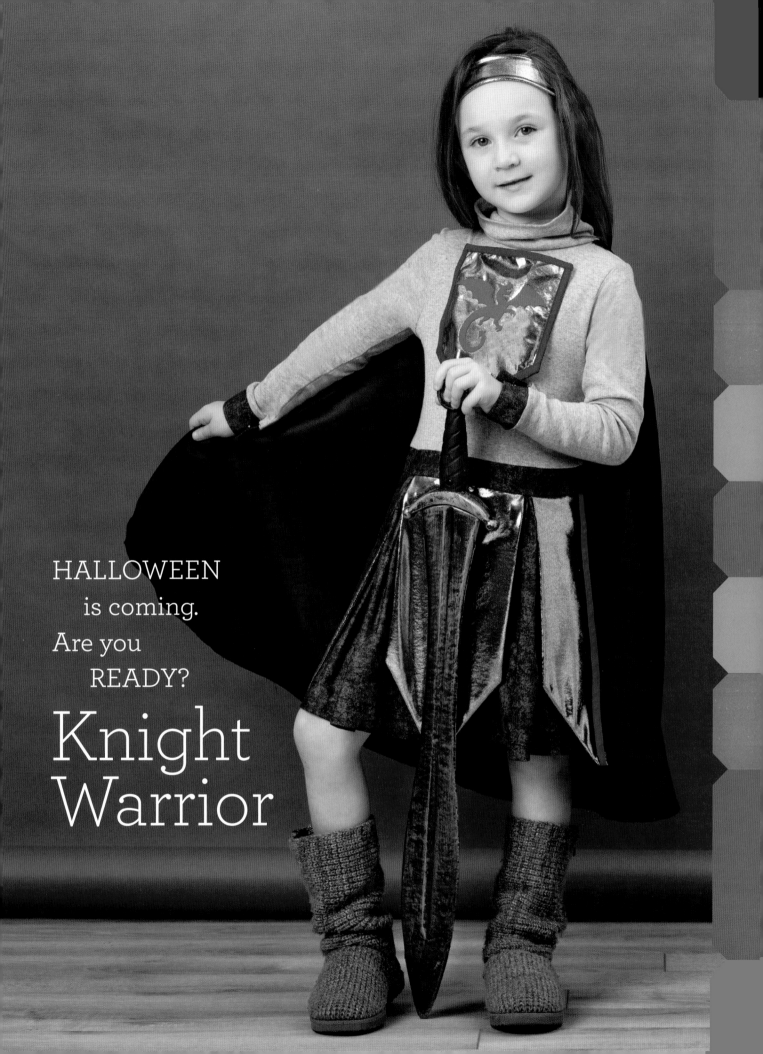

HALLOWEEN
is coming.
Are you
READY?
Knight
Warrior

Knight Warrior

This brave girl is ready for battle in her armor and cape. The armor skirt plates and breast plate only look heavy. Made out of metallic spandex, they will keep her light on her feet.

Instructions are for sizes Small (Medium, Large, Extra-Large). Select the size to sew based on the closest matching chest measurement in the chart on page 6. All seam allowances are ½" unless otherwise noted.

WHAT YOU'LL NEED
- Basic tool kit (see page 7)
- Craft knife
- Narrow-rolled hem foot
- T-shirt: gray, long-sleeve turtleneck
- Two ¼" snaps
- ⅜"-wide red grosgrain ribbon (see yardage chart at right)

For the skirt:
- Distress black print cotton (see yardage chart at right)
- Silver metallic spandex fabric (see yardage chart at right)

For the cape:
- Black microsuede (see yardage at right)
- ½ yard ½"-wide seam binding tape

For the breast plate:
- 14" x 14" lightweight iron-on interfacing
- Red 5" x 5" iron-on twill patch
- Dragon template (page 134)

TIP
Low-tack Scotch tape holds narrow ribbon in place better than pins. It removes easily by pulling toward the sewing seam. Make sure all tape is removed before pressing.

44"-wide fabric	S (2/3)	M (4/5)	L (6/6x)	XL (7/8)
Distress black cotton	1½ yards	1½ yards	1¾ yards	1¾ yards

58"-wide fabric	S (2/3)	M (4/5)	L (6/6x)	XL (7/8)
Black microsuede	¾ yard	¾ yard	1 yard	1 yard
Metallic spandex silver	¾ yard	1 yard	1 yard	1 yard

⅜"-wide ribbon	S (2/3)	M (4/5)	L (6/6x)	XL (7/8)
Red grosgrain	2¾ yards	2¾ yards	3 yards	3½ yards

PREPARING THE T-SHIRT

1. Lay the T-shirt out flat, measure and mark 3½ (4, 4½, 5)" down from each underarm seam, and follow the cutting instructions on page 6. Mark the center front and center back.

SEWING THE BREASTPLATE

2. Cut one 9" x 9" piece each of the black cotton fabric, silver spandex, and the interfacing. On the wrong side of the black fabric, follow the product instructions and iron on the interfacing. Mark the center point of the bottom edge of the square. Measure and mark both side edges 2" up from the bottom. Cut both fabric pieces from the center point to the two outer edge marks to create the pointed bottom of the shield. On the right side of the silver fabric piece, cut five strips of grosgrain ribbon. Lay the strips flat, overlapping at the corners, and sew each ¼" from the edges. With right sides together and using a ¼" seam, sew the silver and black fabric pieces together. Sew next to the ribbon around the four lower edges, leaving the top open. Clip the corners and turn right side out. Press and fold in the top edge. Topstitch around all the edges, closing the top.

3. Copy the dragon template and lightly tape it over the iron-on twill patch. With a sharp craft knife, carefully cut out the appliqué. Place it on the center front of the breastplate and follow the product instructions for pressing time. Handstitch the breastplate to the T-shirt, securing at the corners only.

TRIMMING THE CUFFS

4. Cut 2" off each T-shirt cuff. Cut two pieces of the black fabric. To determine the width, measure the circumference of the T-shirt cuff, then add 2". Cut the length at 4". With right sides together, fold the piece in half lengthwise. Sew a ¼" seam around the cut edges, leaving an open space to turn right side out. Turn right side out, press, and topstitch all four edges. With right sides together and using a narrow zig-zag stitch, sew the cuff to the T-shirt sleeve. Leave a 1" flap to overlap the cuff. Handstitch a snap for the cuff closure.

Knight Warrior

SEWING THE WAISTBAND AND SKIRT ARMOR PLATES

5. To determine the waistband black fabric cutting width, measure the circumference of the T-shirt at the chest and add 2". Cut the waistband length at 5". With right sides facing, sew the short edges together to create the center back seam. Fold in half lengthwise, with wrong sides together, baste-stitch, and then finish-stitch the edges to form a 2½" waistband. Fold the waistband to divide into quarters and mark the sides and front.

6. To make the skirt armor plates, cut four pieces of the black fabric, silver spandex, and interfacing 6" wide by the skirt length measurements in the chart below. On the wrong side of the black fabric, follow the product instructions and iron on the interfacing. Mark the center point of the narrow edge of the rectangle. Measure and mark both side edges 5" up from bottom. With wrong sides of the silver and black fabric together, cut from the center point to the two outer edge marks to create the pointed bottom of the armor plates. On the silver fabric piece, sew the grosgrain ribbon from the point to the center top. With right sides together, sew a ¼" seam along the four lower edges, leaving the top open. Clip the corners and turn right side out. Finish-stitch the top edge closed. Repeat for all four armor plates.

	S (2/3)	M (4/5)	L (6/6x)	XL (7/8)
Skirt length	11"	12"	13"	15"

7. Evenly space and sew the skirt armor plates around the waistband. With right sides together, using a narrow zigzag stitch and matching the sides, front, and back marks, sew the waistband to the T-shirt.

SEWING THE SKIRT

8. Measure the circumference of the T-shirt at the chest and multiply by 2 to determine the skirt fabric cutting width. If the width measurement is wider than the fabric width, divide that number in half. Then cut two fabric pieces and sew them together. This creates two side seams and prevents an awkward seam placement. Use the skirt length chart above to cut the skirt length.

9. Finish-stitch along the top and bottom edges. With right sides facing, fold and sew the sides to make the back seam of the skirt. On the waistline edge, sew two rows of basting stitches for gathering; sew one row ¼" from the edge and the second row ¼" below that. Fold to divide the skirt into quarters and mark the sides, front, and back. Narrow-hem (see page 10) the bottom edge.

ATTACHING THE SKIRT TO THE WAISTBAND

10. Pull the basting threads to gather the skirt waistline. With right sides together, sew the skirt to the waistband, matching the sides, front, and back marks. Remove all the gathering stitches.

SEWING THE CAPE

11. Measure from the shoulder to the hem of the dress, then add 2" for the length of the fabric cutting measurement. Cut the black microsuede fabric according to the chart below for the cape width.

	S (2/3)	M (4/5)	L (6/6x)	XL (7/8)
Cape width	40"	40"	58"	58"

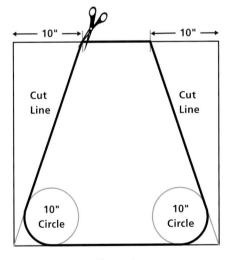

12. As in Figure A, mark along the top edge of the fabric 10" from each side. Cut from each mark to a bottom corner to create a trapezoid shape. Make a 10" circle paper template. Align at the bottom points and cut to round the corners. Use a narrow rolled hem foot to finish all four side edges.

13. On the cape top edge, sew two rows of basting stitches for gathering. Sew one row ¼" from the edge and the second row ¼" below that. Cut a strip of seam binding tape the length measured from the T-shirt shoulder to shoulder outer edges. Pull the basting threads to gather. Divide and position the ruffles to be mostly at the shoulders and smooth across the back of the neck. Sew the cape to the binding tape between the gathering stitch rows.

14. Handstitch the cape across the T-shirt neck and shoulders. Remove all the gathering stitches.

MAKING THE HEADBAND
15. Measure the child's head circumference to determine the cutting width of the silver fabric and cut the length at 5". With right sides together, fold in half and sew along the long edge to create a tube. Turn the tube right side out. Turn a ½" of the fabric edge inside one end of the tube. Tuck the other end inside the tube and sew the back seam. ■

Figure A

Templates

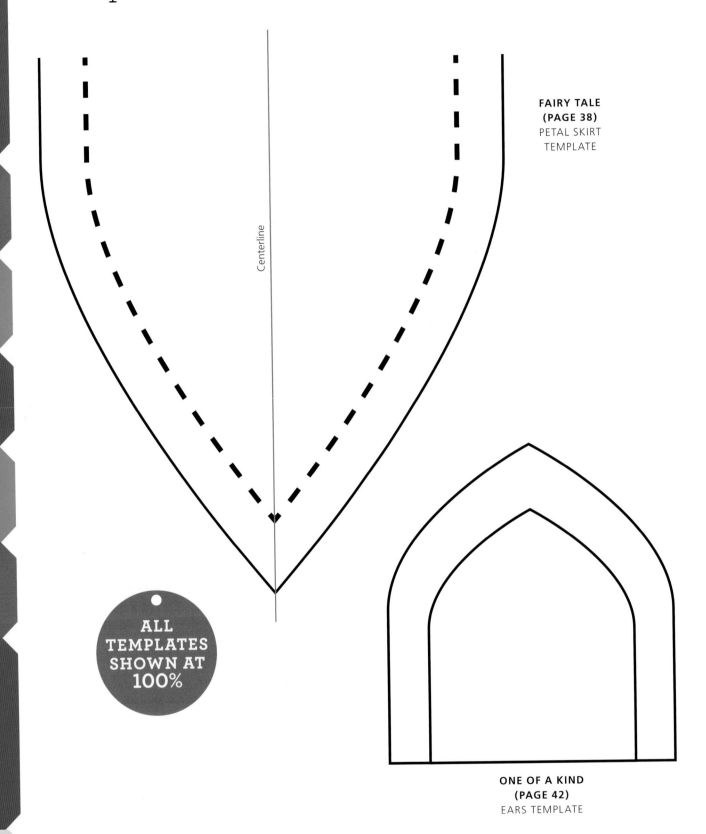

Centerline

**FAIRY TALE
(PAGE 38)**
PETAL SKIRT
TEMPLATE

ALL
TEMPLATES
SHOWN AT
100%

**ONE OF A KIND
(PAGE 42)**
EARS TEMPLATE

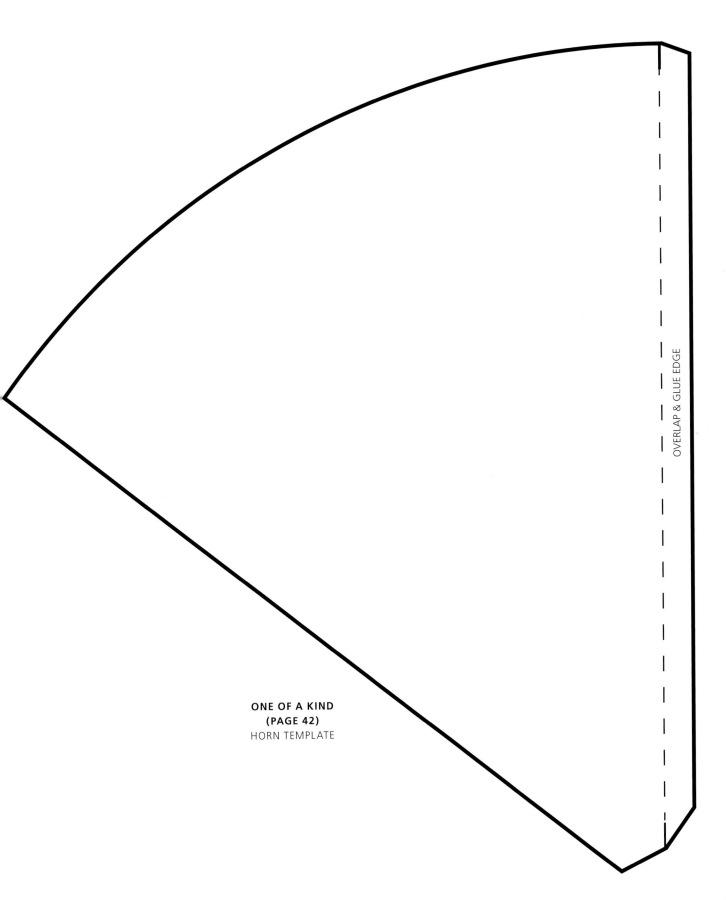

**ONE OF A KIND
(PAGE 42)**
HORN TEMPLATE

OVERLAP & GLUE EDGE

**WILD WEST
(PAGE 52)**
SHERIFF STAR TEMPLATE

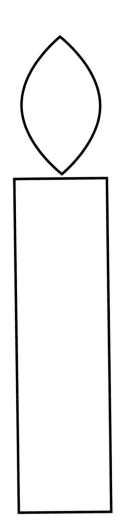

**CELEBRATE!
(PAGE 48)**
BIRTHDAY CANDLE
TEMPLATE

ALL
TEMPLATES
SHOWN AT
100%

**THAT '70S GIRL
(PAGE 56)**
PEACE SIGN TEMPLATE

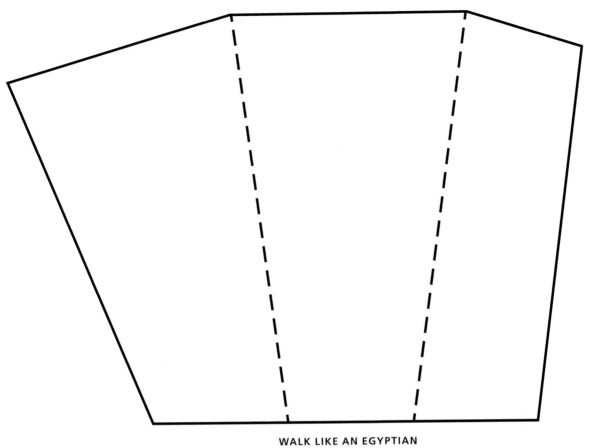

WALK LIKE AN EGYPTIAN
(PAGE 60)
EGYPTIAN MEDALLION TEMPLATE

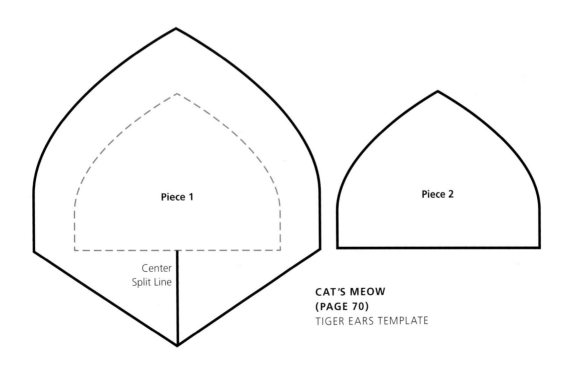

Piece 1

Center
Split Line

Piece 2

CAT'S MEOW
(PAGE 70)
TIGER EARS TEMPLATE

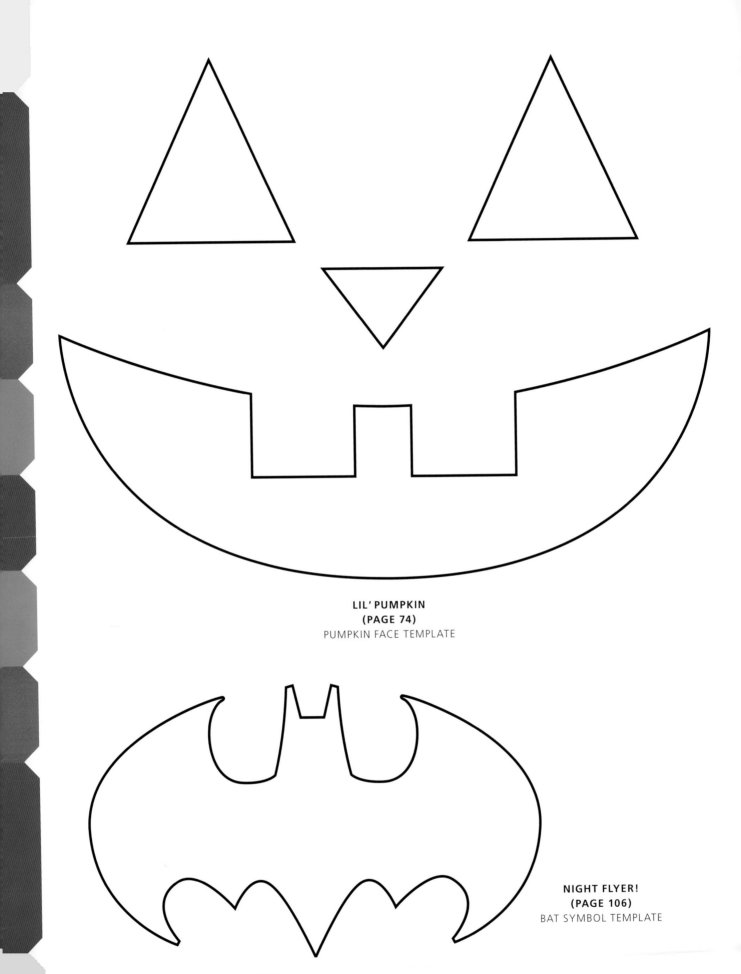

**LIL' PUMPKIN
(PAGE 74)**
PUMPKIN FACE TEMPLATE

**NIGHT FLYER!
(PAGE 106)**
BAT SYMBOL TEMPLATE

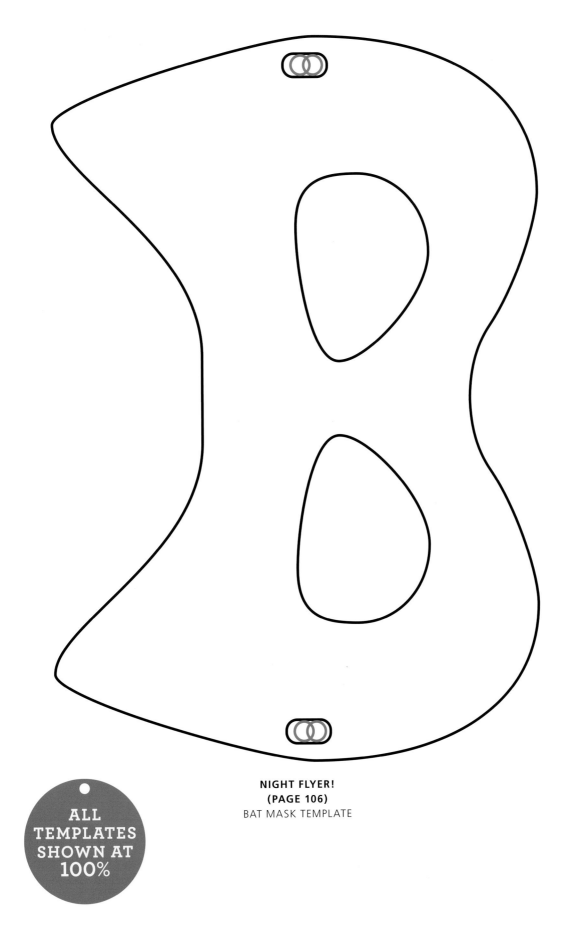

NIGHT FLYER!
(PAGE 106)
BAT MASK TEMPLATE

GIRL POWER!
(PAGE 118)
SUPERHERO STAR TEMPLATE

ALL TEMPLATES SHOWN AT 100%

KNIGHT WARRIOR
(PAGE 123)
DRAGON TEMPLATE

ROYAL TREATMENT
(PAGE 12)

MEASUREMENT CONVERSION CHART
YARDS TO INCHES TO METERS

YARDS	INCHES	METERS
⅛	4.5	.11
¼	9	.23
⅜	13.5	.34
½	18	.46
⅝	22.5	.57
¾	27	.69
⅞	31.5	.80
1	36	.91
1⅛	40.5	1.03
1¼	45	1.14
1⅜	49.5	1.26
1½	54	1.37
1⅝	58.5	1.49
1¾	63	1.60
1⅞	67.5	1.71
2	72	1.83

1 INCH = 2.540 CENTIMETERS

1 YARD = .9144 METERS

1 CENTIMETER = .3937 INCHES

1 METER = 3.281 FEET/1.094 YARDS

Index

CELEBRATE!
(PAGE 48)

BUSY BEE
(PAGE 96)

**LITTLE RED
(PAGE 33)**

Index (cont.)

**ONE OF
A KIND
(PAGE 42)**